SERVING JUSTICE

SERVING JUSTICE

A Supreme Court Clerk's View

J. Harvie Wilkinson, III

Charterhouse

NEW YORK

Serving Justice

LIBRARY OF CONGRESS CATALOG CARD NUMBER: 74–78898
ISBN: 0–88327–044–7
MANUFACTURED IN THE UNITED STATES OF AMERICA

To
Lossie

FOREWORD

This happy combination of charm, information, and ideas is the work of a young man who will be making valuable contributions to the worlds of legal and historical thought for years to come. Those of us who have been studying the Supreme Court since before the author was born will gain from reading him. Those coming to him as students, whether in the schools or outside them, can benefit immeasurably.

Mr. Wilkinson is a graduate of Yale College and the University of Virginia Law School, where he now teaches. Upon graduation from law school, he spent two years as a clerk to Justice Lewis F. Powell of the Supreme Court. Both modestly and accurately, he perceives that he gained that position by a mix of geographic propinquity and personal acquaintance. He brought to his year at the Court diligence, perceptiveness, and principle, all of which are reflected in this volume growing out of his experience.

The author reports on three main subjects. The first

is law clerks: how they are chosen, what they do, their place in the scheme of things. The second is a chapter on Powell himself. Third is a discussion of the Court and its place in American life, with particular attention to the Court headed by Chief Justice Burger, the Court which the author by personal observation knew best.

Anyone who wishes to know about these things will benefit from reading Mr. Wilkinson. As a source on Justice Powell, he will from this day forward be indispensable, for he has done a superb job of compressing the facts and spirit of a remarkable figure into short compass. On the other two topics, he has much that is valuable to say.

The impending, if not the present, crisis of the Supreme Court in our time is its rising work load. There are differences among the Justices as to whether the Court can comfortably and adequately handle the load it now has, but there is scarcely room to doubt that with the inevitably increasing load, the only alternatives are radically changed procedures—or breakdown. Wilkinson reminds us of the pointed and valid remarks of Justice Powell at the Fourth Circuit to the general effect that no senior partner of a large American law office would expect to put up with the kind of inadequate staffing and assistance of a Supreme Court Justice.

One possibility is greatly to increase staff, a view which able and conscientious judges and commentators around the country have espoused. Wilkinson is not ready to embrace the view that any great increase in the number of law clerks would be at all desirable.

Some typists and some paralegals would be useful, but for a Justice Powell, who is firmly determined to be (as he ought to be) his own judge, a significant increase in useful clerks would be a mixed blessing. Properly used (and Wilkinson discusses their proper use) clerks are learners, companions, and useful aides; but they are no substitute for a Justice. When I was a law clerk to Justice Black more than thirty years ago, my Justice made some thousand decisions in the course of a year, and I am happy to say that I never affected any of them.

This chapter vividly carries through that tradition of the clerk as aide but by no means as judge-substitute. Justice Rehnquist as a young man and an ex–law clerk once wrote a somewhat overheated piece on what he thought was the excessive influence of the clerks toward liberalism in the Court. Wilkinson, perhaps unnecessarily, gives considerable answer to this concern; it is doubtful that Rehnquist the Justice, his own man if ever there was one, still finds much cause for worry in this quarter.

Wilkinson came to the Court deeply interested in Chief Justice Warren and the Court over which he presided, an interest which has grown with such casual personal interchanges as they have had subsequently. Hence, he is properly thoughtful over the relation, in the historical continuum, of the Burger court, with which he was associated, to its great predecessor. He legitimately decries the conception of a Nixon bloc, insofar as this somewhat invidious term suggests some common quarterback calling signals. At the same time, he recognizes that an administration seeking

fundamentally like-minded though completely independent appointees has basically found them. In the
course of his discussion he creates a miniature bio-
graphical trove of illuminating passages on several of
the Justices. He finds no Nixon counterrevolution following the Warren period, though he has a clear sense
of what has been well described by others as the Nixon
pause.

There is an irregular rhythm in the dynamics of the
Supreme Court. Between the great flush of excitement
of the rising New Deal and the Warren period came
what I described in an essay on the Chief Justiceship
of Fred Vinson as the Passive Period. As Wilkinson
demonstrates, the current years are not a time of a
total passivity, but they are much closer to it than the
Warren era. There have not been any desegregation
or any one-man, one-vote decisions lately. Wilkinson
finds a comfortable analogy to the present course of
decision in Beethoven's Fourth Symphony, "a beautiful and serene peace between the more boisterous
themes of the 3rd and the 5th." All the same, if Beethoven had not composed the Third, Fifth, Seventh
and Ninth symphonies, it is not very likely that the
Fourth would get much attention today.

For me, there is a pleasant sense of closing a personal circle in welcoming Mr. Wilkinson's book to the
shelves of Supreme Court literature. Justice Powell
succeeded Justice Black. In 1942, I went to work as
Black's clerk in the identical suite which Powell oc-
cupied when Wilkinson arrived. The redoubtable
Spencer Campbell was messenger for both. As the
excellent chapter on Powell makes clear, the connection is more than one of space and personnel. Like

Black, Powell is an indefatigable worker, a warm and generous man, and an independent spirit.

John P. Frank
Phoenix, Arizona

May, 1974

ACKNOWLEDGMENTS

During the 1971 and 1972 terms of the Supreme Court I served as a law clerk to Justice Lewis F. Powell, Jr. The experience was a rewarding one in many different ways, and yet, while there, I was troubled by the misunderstanding and distrust that sometimes characterized public reaction to the Court's work. My aim in this book is to provide a brief personal view and an understanding of the Supreme Court that developed during the time that I worked there.

Much of what goes on within the Supreme Court must be kept in confidence if the spirit of frank and informal exchange there is to continue to prevail. The need for such confidence in the Court's deliberations will always be important, and I have tried in every instance to respect it.

Several colleagues at the University of Virginia Law School have been most helpful in the preparation of this book. Professors Daniel J. Meador and A. E. Dick Howard, both clerks for the late Justice Hugo Black, read the manuscript and made needed suggestions. Stephen Saltzburg, clerk to Justice Thurgood Marshall for the 1971 term, provided thoughtful reactions to my own impressions. Because each clerk's recollections of the Supreme Court are different and quite personal, these persons should not be charged with any of the views stated herein.

My father gave the manuscript his usual frank and unsparing critique, for which I am—in the long run—always grateful. Michael DeCamps, my student assistant at the law school, was invaluable in research and final preparation of the manuscript. Diane Moss and the Publications Office did excellent typing on very short notice.

To Sterling Lord, my agent, and Richard Kluger, former publisher of Charterhouse, go my sincere thanks for suggesting and encouraging this undertaking. And Carol Rinzler, now head of Charterhouse, has proved the kind of friend and critic for whom any author would have been grateful.

CONTENTS

1

THE ACCEPTANCE

For the first twenty years of my life I never knew what a Supreme Court law clerk was. For the next five, I never thought or hoped to be one. But it happened, and for the rest of my life, I will be grateful that it did.

"You have nothing to lose by applying" was my professor's offhand remark in the hallway at the University of Virginia, where I was in my last year of law school. "If I were you, I'd give it a fling." Later I stopped by his office to ask if he were serious. Hadn't Supreme Court clerkships been dominated by Harvard and Yale law graduates? I asked. Yes, he replied, but that was somewhat less true today than in the past. "They [the Justices] don't discriminate against Southerners," he laughed. But I had not been at the top of my class, and my record contained telltale evidence of missing motivation. "Don't get your hopes up," he agreed. "It's an incredible longshot. But you ought to apply."

I left, promising to think it over. That evening I

1

phoned a friend of the family, Lewis F. Powell, Jr., then a partner at the Richmond law firm of Hunton, Williams, Gay, Powell and Gibson, and someone who had always been generous with his interest and advice. My first summer job, back in high school, had been for his law firm. I was then a messenger; I sharpened pencils, collected mail, and shuttled paperwork among the lawyers for thirty-five dollars a week. At the end of the summer he congratulated me. "One day you may make a good lawyer," he said. But how did carrying papers from one office to another relate to law? I wondered. His answer had to do with pride in one's job.

After that summer Mr. Powell had kept in touch. I remember one particular thing he said right after my sophomore year at Yale. He had learned, he said, of my grades from my father and had not been pleased. He could not escape the impression that I was going through college as if there were no tomorrow. I very quickly got the point. His message, I later told him, had a serious chilling effect on my collegiate fun.

We had not had much chance to talk at length since then, but, for some reason, when it came time for decision, I turned to him for advice. Now the voice at the other end of the phone unhesitatingly urged me to apply for a Supreme Court clerkship. "You won't regret it," he said. "It's a great experience. I would like to have been one myself." Then, after a pause, "Of course, there are hundreds of applicants. But if you like, I will write you a recommendation." That suggestion I accepted happily.

A Supreme Court clerkship normally lasts one year, during which time the clerk assists a particular Justice in his legal research and work. His three clerks comprise a Justice's entire legal staff. Applicants for a clerkship routinely apply to many Justices, in my case four.

Having decided to apply, I began to think more about what kind of institution the Supreme Court might be. One vivid impression dated ironically from an experience in politics. In 1970 I had been the Republican nominee in a humblingly unsuccessful campaign for Congress in Virginia's third district. The campaign trail, full of shopping centers, factory gates, midmorning coffees, and evening debates, is arduous and especially difficult for nonincumbents. Yet it was a worthwhile experience. As a candidate, I received a tumble of impressions about Vietnam, inflation, the crime and drug problems, or whatever people had most on their minds. The dominant issue of the campaign, however, was that of busing students to desegregate the public schools. A federal district judge had decreed for Richmond, Virginia, a plan of extensive crosscity transportation, and a great many voters, especially parents, were upset. Both my opponent and I saw little sense in the plan. In one way, however, our whole debate on the subject was a charade, so completely had the issue been taken over by the courts. Voters sensed this and became the more frustrated that an issue that touched the well-being of their children was beyond their power to influence. Late one afternoon, at the state fairgrounds, three men and I were talking. "Just tell me one thing," the first asked, "how in the heck does something like this get taken from the people and put in the hands of the Supreme Court?"

After the election I returned to law school. From my venture into politics I believed the Supreme Court had come to be too powerful an instrument in an elective society. But law school imparts different impressions. There, very subtly, the great judges—Benjamin Cardozo, Learned Hand, Roger Traynor—become near gods, and one gradually learned the judicial faith.

Among the most powerful presences at a law school are those of the great Supreme Court Justices, among them during my years there Hugo Black and John M. Harlan. Now in their later years, they were giants of the Court. Harlan, despite descending blindness, remained the supreme legal craftsman; Black, still zestful in his eighties, lived to watch many early dissents become law. So much of the Supreme Court story can be told through their contrasting views and styles: Black, the symbol of clarion simplicity in the law; Harlan, its master of refinement and nuance. Black, who sought from the venerable words of the Constitution a strict and binding Bible for judges; Harlan, who saw judges as restrained but conscientious interpreters of evolving standards of fairness in society. Black, the great voice for a national Bill of Rights; Harlan, the champion of pluralistic federalism and state experimentation. Black, an absolute defender of free speech; Harlan, a sensitive First Amendment balancer of public interests and personal rights. Their battles mesmerized me, often to the detriment of other law school courses. I thought they must have been close personally and shared the respect that honest and profound antagonisms bring.

Justices Harlan and Black were two to whom I had hoped to apply. I had, by chance, known several of

Justice Black's former clerks. Listening to them, I felt the experience that clerking for him must have been. Justice Black had hit them like Pauls toward Damascus: They had emerged into the world rededicated, not entirely their old selves again. They told stories of bridge and tennis with "the Judge," as his clerks called him, and for his eightieth birthday the clerks had printed a small pamphlet entitled *Confessions of the Law Clerks,* a story of association with a man of vision, conviction, and vigor, capped by a boundless sense of mischief and fun. His tennis exploits were especially legendary; many of his clerks were superlative players, but not all:

> He told me to bring my racquet and come out to his house and play tennis. And I told him, "Judge, I can't play tennis." And he said, "Don't you own a tennis racquet?" And I said, "Yes sir." And he said, "Well, you play tennis and are being modest." And I said, "No, sir; I'm being truthful." And he said, "Well, I've seen this before, so get your racquet and come on out." So I did, and boy, I was miserable. He said, "You are truthful after all."
>
> A couple of days later he said, "What are you doing Saturday morning?" And I said, "Well, I was going to come in here and work on cert petitions." And he said, "You are reporting for duty to the tennis pro at the Army-Navy Country Club." And he sent me out to take lessons.[1]

Suddenly, in the fall of 1971, Justices Black and Harlan died. The shock of such a double tragedy was enormous. Many must have agreed with Philip Kurland, Professor of Law at the University of Chicago, who mourned the departure of the two men because it deprived the Court "of the same quality—the quality of quality," and predicted: "No matter who the replacements, the Supreme Court is likely to be a sadly debilitated institution for some years to come."[2] I felt saddened, perhaps selfishly so. I had neither met the two Justices nor known them save through their opinions and the stories of their law clerks, but I felt I vaguely understood their loss and wondered whether, without them, the Supreme Court would be a less vibrant and exhilarating place. For a moment I considered abandoning my whole effort.

But not for long. Justices Byron White and Potter Stewart, in response to my applications, had asked me to the Supreme Court for interviews. This did not mean I had a job, however. It did indicate, I presumed, that each Justice had narrowed the field to maybe ten or fifteen serious applicants. From my experience at law school I had come to think of an interview as an amiable, if somewhat tedious, exercise, designed by the law firm to test such things as good grooming and client compatibility. Nothing much would be accomplished beyond a rough impression of how the two principals hit it off. Thus I was startled when, instead of the usual rambling preliminaries, Justice White began, very intently, to question me in searching terms about my views of the Supreme Court. An answer only provoked more questions, and I sat before him, responding as best I could, not knowing what he thought or whether he agreed. After roughly a half hour, I left, intrigued and quite stimulated, but unsure

6

of what impression, if any, I had made.

Justice Stewart was more low-key. We had both gone to Yale as undergraduates, and he appeared interested in the views of a more recent alumnus. I felt easy and welcome in his presence, as if we had a range of common interests and, in fact, we had discovered several mutual friends.

Driving back to law school, I was certain I had botched it. There was no way to have prepared for Justice White. I mulled over all the silly answers I was sure I had given him and kicked myself for not responding thoughtfully. The two Justices had seemed so very different to me and yet, as I told a classmate upon my return, I would have given my eyeteeth for a clerkship with either one.

Several days later Justice Stewart wrote that he had decided on someone else. Although Justice White had not yet chosen, I was not optimistic and thought it prudent to consider other plans upon leaving law school. As graduation neared, I plunged into final examinations and study for the bar, the thought of a clerkship now well back in my mind.

One evening some friends asked me to dinner, after which we were to listen to President Nixon formally nominate the successors to Justices Black and Harlan. It was not a bright prospect. The names of Mildred Lillie and Herschel Friday were circulating, to the acute dismay of much of the legal profession and those who followed the Supreme Court. The idea that two of the Court's greats would meet such replacement disturbed me deeply. I slumped in front of the television, prepared for the worst.

Nixon's speech had a long preamble. The President

talked studiedly about the greatness of the Supreme Court, deliberately building suspense. "The Supreme Court is the highest judicial body in this country. Its members, therefore, should, above all, be among the very best lawyers in the nation." The emphasis on excellence made me suspect that Lillie and maybe Friday had been discarded, but as to his final choices, the President as yet gave no clue. There was only the familiar caution that judges should "interpret" the Constitution, not "twist or bend" it, and his own determination to give "the peace forces" the "legal tools they need to protect the innocent from criminal elements." Finally, summoning his most earnest air, Mr. Nixon got down to business:

> It is with these criteria in mind that I have selected the two men whose names I will send to the Senate tomorrow. Everything that Lewis F. Powell has undertaken he has accomplished with distinction and honor.[3]

"Lewis Powell!" The Supreme Court had, I felt, been saved and along with it, I could not help thinking, my chances for a clerkship! My jubilation just about turned over my friends' coffee table. But wait, I thought . . . suppose he were not confirmed? Suppose all of Justice Black's clerks asked to stay on, and there were no opening? Suppose he preferred to work with someone he had not previously known? Or someone with prior clerking experience? I could do nothing but sit tight.

But the confirmation proceeded smoothly. There was general relief at the sight of two qualified nomi-

8

nees, and William Rehnquist, as the younger and seemingly more "conservative," took most of the heat. On December 6, 1971, Lewis F. Powell, Jr., was confirmed as the ninety-ninth Justice in the history of the United States Supreme Court. "Dear Jay," his letter to me began. "I have ascertained that one of Mr. Justice Black's three clerks will not remain at the Court after the first of the year. Accordingly, ..." Already I had begun writing my acceptance.

2
THE CLERK

I arrived for work on Monday, February 7, 1972. Several weeks before, I had been just a graduating law student cramming for final exams and to pass the bar. Now, on approaching the United States Supreme Court, I felt myself suddenly and mistakenly hurtled to some remote height where I had no earthly business being. My first view of the Supreme Court only confirmed this: the building, with massive, sculptured forms of Justice and Liberty flanking the entrance and lofty exterior columns of bone-white marble, projected infallibility, though it housed men who, as Justice William Brennan once put it, live and work with the awareness "that their best may not be equal to the challenge."[1]

Inside, the Supreme Court seemed a maze of marble corridors, each one like every other. Much of my first few days there were spent simply mastering directions. Once, while trying to find Justice Marshall's chambers, I ended twice at Justice Blackmun's. Walking these corridors, threading crowds of omnipresent tourists, I was moved to be working in a place so many came so far to see. I marveled also that I was now in a place I had been reading about, studying about, defending or lamenting these past three years. Now finally I would be watching the distant names become flesh figures and discovering that a myriad of human dilemmas and emotions, so much a part of the outside world, also found their way in here.

The time of my arrival no doubt heightened such first impressions. The term of the Supreme Court formally begins early in October and normally ends in middle or late June of the next year. Most new law clerks arrive in July or early August and have a month or two to acquaint themselves with Court procedures and upcoming cases. Because of the date of Justice Powell's appointment, however, I came right at midterm, with the Court in full swing. Work, in the form of briefs and petitions piled high on my desk, greeted my arrival. The Supreme Court is "reflection in action," a fellow clerk once told me, somehow capturing in that offhand observation an institutional irony I was never to forget. Those first days I yearned often for more reflection and less action. They were days of frustration and mistake that brought to me the recurring image of running desperately to catch some departing train that was always pulling slowly and agonizingly out of sight.

Justice Powell had temporarily inherited the chambers of Justice Hugo Black. His chambers, in the far northeast corner of the building, consisted of three oak-paneled rooms—a large corner office for the Justice himself, on either side of which was an office for his secretary and one for his law clerks. The chambers still bore remembrances of its late occupant: the law books had Hugo Black's signature stamped on their pages, and the cart on which Justice Powell's legal memoranda were wheeled to conference with his fellow Justices still had Justice Black's name painted on the side. More vivid was the presence of Spencer Campbell, Justice Black's aging messenger, who had been with him in his days as a United States Senator, and throughout his thirty-four years on the Supreme Court. The messenger's function dates back from the time when Justices worked in their own homes. Today, with all the Justices working at the Court, the messenger maintains files, carries copies of a Justice's draft opinions and other memoranda around to other chambers, and acts as general handyman. At sixty-three short, slim, and slightly stooped, Spencer carried an easy smile and manner and an astonishing wealth of lore about the Court and Justices present and past. His years with Justice Black made him something of an expert on office procedures, and Justice Powell gladly rehired him.

Such reminders of Justice Black were in turn reminders of the continuity and durability of the institution. For Justice Black had served with Justice Louis D. Brandeis, who had served with Justice Oliver Wendell Holmes, who in turn had served with the first Justice John M. Harlan, and so on through the great names of the past, like some solemn torchlight procession treading back across the life of the nation. In the more immediate sense of continuity, two of Justice Black's most recent law clerks had stayed on after his death to assist whomever might be his successor. Pete Parnell had grown up in Alabama, had graduated from Harvard Law School, and clerked for Judge Francis Van Dusen of the Third Circuit Court of Appeals before being chosen by Justice Black; while Larry Hammond came from the University of Texas and a year with Judge Carl McGowan on the District of Columbia Circuit Court. It could not have been much fun for them to have a novice law clerk interrupt their own work every ten minutes with a question. They bore me, however, with remarkable patience and humor and generally helped the chambers settle in. Pete left at the end of the 1971 session to practice law in Los Angeles, while Larry remained with Justice Powell for the following term.

Anchor of our chambers was Sally Smith, the Justice's personal secretary. Sally some years ago left teaching grade school in Winchester, Virginia, to become a legal secretary, to be, as she put it, "where the action was." She came to Richmond, found a job with Justice Powell's firm, and not long afterward became his secretary. When the nomination came, Sally, with the Justice, stood the deluge, sorting thousands of congratulatory letters, processing floods of clerkship applications, fielding requests from the press for interviews, from the Senate Judiciary Committee for the nominee's past statements, and finally assisting her boss's windup of a large private practice in Richmond and the move to a Supreme Court judgeship. Needless to say, when the move came, Sally made it also.

In Washington she lived only a block from the Justice, and would drive him to and from work each day. At the office she was the discreet and efficient secretary, but pulled me short with quick lines, inquiring on certain days why I had bothered even to get up, and once terming one of my memoranda to the Justice "a fine piece of soap opera. We've got to book this boy on *Queen for a Day.*" She was unflappable in the face of work or adversity, typing six or seven drafts of an opinion without a wince. When the Court entered its final sprint from April to the term's end in June, she routinely worked a seven-day week, bringing the Justice his weekend hamburgers "well-done, please, Sally, with just a touch of mustard."

Among the Supreme Court's many Washington Redskin fans, Sally Smith is the premiere, an ancient season ticket holder. She asked me once to a Monday night game between the Redskins and the Atlanta Falcons. It was late November, low temperatures and freezing winds swept the stadium, and midway through the third quarter I hinted that the Redskins had the contest and might it not be nice to go home. Sally, who by then was only beginning to warm to the game, company, and refreshments, shook her head: "Jay, when are you going to learn what's a good party?"

The size of the personal staff of an Associate Justice of the Supreme Court is typically quite small. During my first term as a clerk most chambers consisted of six persons: the Justice himself, a personal secretary, a messenger, and three law clerks. Beginning with the 1972 term most Justices added a second secretary, but staff size remained a far cry from offices in the lower House of Congress, for example, which may hire up to sixteen. When I first came to work, quarters were cramped: three law clerks shared the same, rather small room, reading, talking, typing together, a wonderful climate for camaraderie if not always for work. The 1972 term brought an improvement in that condition also; rearrangement of space within the Court gave most chambers a fourth room or the chance to enlarge one or more of the existing three.

The small size and staff of each Justice's chambers is one of the Supreme Court's most distinctive features. It gave to Justice Powell's chambers, as I believe it did to others, a sense of unity and compactness, the feeling of being harnessed together that was necessary to accomplish the arduous job of research and analysis a Supreme Court case frequently requires. It made possible a collective pride in the quality of legal work produced by the chambers as well as a rivalry among individual chambers even as they worked in the larger sense together. It encouraged within our own chambers frank and often heated debate on many a legal issue that would have become diffused and less vital in a more formal setting or among larger numbers. I spent many hours with fellow Powell clerks hacking and sawing at one another's ideas or, equally as often, helping or being helped over a difficult hump.

Justice Brandeis is supposed to have commented that "However much one could criticize the Supreme Court of the United States, it endured and deserved its place in our political structure because it did its own work."[2] His comment illustrates how much is owed to the small chamber size that allows a Justice to concentrate directly on the Court's cases, free of administrative obligations to set lines of supervision and responsibility among a large staff. Often, while thinking of the problems of Watergate, I would gratefully compare the structure at the Supreme Court with that of the executive branch. No member of a six-man staff wanders easily from the Justice's personal attention or direction. Important judgment calls are less likely to get lost in the administrative machinery or delegated very far from the Justice's personal supervision.

But the small and intimate atmosphere of the chambers also had its unattractive side. Upon arrival at the Supreme Court, Justice Powell found that "perhaps the single greatest shock to me personally" was the inadequacy of available resources.

> I have an office suite of only three rooms. I have one secretary, who serves as file clerk, reception-ist, as well as a highly confidential personal secre-tary. . . . My three law clerks are crowded into a single small room, each doing his own typing in the absence of secretarial help. . . .
>
> There is no permanent legal staff available to the Court; no experienced lawyers to call on; and no one to do protracted and scholarly research— beyond the basic legal research—under the direc-tion of a Justice. In short, each Justice is on his own, with resources—both physical and in per-sonnel—far less adequate than those of a partner in a well-organized law firm.[3]

I felt, while I was clerking there, that the Supreme Court was standing at something of a crossroads. On the one hand was the charming traditional vision of a Justice deeply steeped in his own work, thinking through ideas and theories by the fireside of his cham-bers with a small and dedicated personal staff. This traditional side of the Court will resist growth and bureaucracy and summon the image of an institution whose greatness lies in the quality and conscientiousness of its personnel, not in its numbers. But against this are the country's legal problems, more numerous, diverse, complex than even a decade ago, and the fact that the modern Supreme Court has taken a more active hand in solving them. Among the many vexing challenges facing the Court is whether and how its valued personalized character can survive the more clamorous legal landscape the future almost surely will bring.

My first duty as a law clerk was to write for Justice Powell memoranda summarizing what lawyers call "petitions for certiorari." The phrase has a complex and formidable ring, but it is nothing more than a request by a party that the Supreme Court hear and decide his case. Since 1925 the Supreme Court has been almost uniquely blessed among the federal courts in being able to select, for the most part, just what cases it will and will not hear. Some such power is essential to the exercise of the high Court's mission to resolve only significant issues of federal law and constitutional policy and to exclude the literally millions of legal contests whose impact extends little farther than the parties with whom they came to court.

This business of deciding what to decide ranks among the Court's most crucial functions. Its very selection of particular kinds of issues commands public attention, irrespective of the Court's final decision on them. Recently this has been a more time-consuming business as well. The total number of certiorari petitions filed with the Supreme Court in 1951 was 1,234; by 1961 there were 2,185, and by the 1971 term 3,643 new cases were filed—an increase in twenty years of nearly 300 percent.[4] These raw figures do not mean that the Justices sat down, for example, during the 1971 term and collectively considered whether to grant a hearing to some 3,600 cases. As Justice Brennan has noted, only about 30 percent of the certiorari petitions raise questions that even a single Justice finds sufficiently meritorious to request discussion by the entire Court. Some petitions present issues a Justice finds wholly unsuitable for Supreme Court review, and he dismisses them very quickly. Justice Brennan gives two good examples: "Are Negroes in fact Indians and therefore entitled to Indians' exemptions from federal income taxes?" and "Does a ban on drivers turning right on a red light constitute an unreasonable burden on interstate commerce?"[5]

Copies of some seventy or eighty petitions for certiorari are circulated each week to the nine chambers, each of which handles them somewhat differently and as it sees fit.[6] One classic procedure is for a Justice to have a clerk type him a memorandum of from one to five pages on every petition, setting forth the factual background to the case, the rulings of the lower courts and their reasoning, the contentions of the parties as to why the Supreme Court should or should not hear the case, and, finally, the clerk's own recommendation as to whether certiorari should be granted. Needless to say, this recommendation might or might not be followed. A former law clerk to Justice Black remembers "one day the Justice coming back from the conference room and telling us what the votes were on the various cases. He reported with great glee on a particular case virtually all the justices' law clerks thought they ought to hear—it was a draft case or something like that—all the Justices had disagreed and unanimously decided not to hear it. He concluded with great pleasure, 'Today the Justices beat the law clerks.' "[7]

I always thought the grant or denial of certiorari to be the Supreme Court's single most misunderstood act. Public discussion of the Supreme Court too frequently confuses the Court's decision merely to hear a case, that is, to grant certiorari, with the final decision of the case itself. In fact, however, the two actions could not be more different. A minority of any four Justices may have a case heard, but a majority vote of five is usually required to decide the very same case. Unlike final decision on a case, the votes and reasons for a grant or denial of certiorari are generally not made public, and action on certiorari is, again unlike a final decision, a most treacherous clue to the Court's real mind.

Justice Harlan once described the question of whether certiorari should be granted as frequently "more a matter of 'feel' than of precisely ascertainable rules,"[8] a more intuitive process than the deliberations preceding final decision. A Justice's votes to grant or deny certiorari can be mysterious and very personal: he may vote to deny certiorari because he thinks the question one of local and not national significance or because the case presents some procedural flaw or too murky and uncertain a set of facts on which to rest an important legal judgment. Although a Justice may eventually want the Court to settle a given issue, he may also want to deny certiorari for the time being, perhaps to give the lower courts and legal scholars an opportunity to provide more input or to give public opinion time to become receptive to what he suspects will be the Court's ultimate ruling. Finally, a Justice may even vote to deny certiorari and leave standing a lower-court ruling he found clearly wrong, rather than risk having the "bad law" affirmed with the seal and approval of the nation's highest court.

I recall with some embarrassment my first certiorari experience with Justice Powell. The case involved the Federal Bankruptcy Act, and bankruptcy had been one course I had studiously avoided ever taking in law school. Now was I, in such untutored state, to write a Supreme Court Justice a memorandum on some aspect of the Bankruptcy Act? He'd wonder what kind of clerk he'd hired. I panicked. But I did what I had done on math exams in high school—put that first perplexing problem aside. But my second petition had to do with an even more complex problem of federal taxation—the one area I knew less about than bankruptcy. Soon my confidence vanished. I slumped at my desk, defeated and self-pitying. Fortunately, a fellow clerk approached. "Don't just sit there," he chided. "One thing you learn here is to keep moving." That at least got me started.

A Supreme Court clerkship is very much a baptism by fire. Doing twenty to thirty cert memos a week, a clerk is quickly compelled to develop a knack for stating the salient facts and issues in a case and a sixth sense for the particular kinds of questions his Justice will be looking for. Before too long Justice Powell was able to write a friend that my cert memos were adequate, "although I must say that his typing leaves a good bit to be desired!" (He dared me once to type ten consecutive words without an error.)

After five months as a clerk I estimated I had typed Justice Powell over one thousand pages of cert notes, something roughly comparable—in bulk only—to *War and Peace*. Reading and summarizing literally hundreds upon hundreds of petitions for certiorari was at times the most tedious of jobs, but it provided me with a frontline, rapid-fire view of all the diverse and multitudinous problems people expect the Supreme Court to hear. So many different matters come before the Court that no single lawyer, however brilliant or versatile, could possibly be knowledgeable on all of them. Antitrust, tax, labor, admiralty, securities, patent, bankruptcy, and an inexhaustible variety of criminal and constitutional claims press upon it. Justices are asked to rule on welfare systems, environmental regulations, school desegregation, legislative reapportionment, sex discrimination, educational finance, prison administration, abortion practice, and other equally far-flung and disparate subjects. For the Supreme Court is one institution that has not been allowed to specialize. Changes in American life and government have only brought the Court a wider, more diverse role than it had a hundred, twenty, even ten years ago. Unlike the system in Congress, no committees and subcommittees exist to help a Justice narrow his interests. Thus, even the most restrained and cautious Justice ends up sounding occasionally like a philosopher, historian, educator, economist—a periodic practitioner of nonlawyerly disciplines. For me, this was at once the Court's bane and redemption, this concept of nine, life-tenured men whose broad, inexpert wisdom roams so pervasively over the problems and conflicts of American life. In fond and agreeing moments I could believe them some transfigured panel of philosopher kings; in others, misguided figures we might all do without.

The range and diversity of the Supreme Court's task stems largely from its "paid" filings, or those petitions where the parties had sufficient funds to submit them to the Court in printed form. But at least half of all the petitioners to the Court are destitute criminal defendants who come, often without legal help, advancing half coherent, hand-scrawled claims. These claims, far from ranging broadly, center almost exclusively on the Fourth, Fifth, and Sixth Amendments to the Constitution and assume, for the most part, a dreary predictability.

One man contends he had not been given *Miranda* warnings; another alleges he was tried by a racially biased jury; a third was denied counsel at preliminary hearing; a fourth was convicted by means of evidence illegally seized by the police. Most of these claims crumble under scrutiny, and the Justices will hear only the tiniest fraction of them. But they pound the Court at a furious pace, indistinguishable voices pleading for relief. Sometimes, despite myself, I would forget they were people and think of them only as names on a legal page, parts of some abstract mental encounter, unrelated to anything real, to human agony, jails, victims, all the groaning that goes on outside. Patience and tolerance yielded too readily to a desire to be done. People became simply items to type up quickly, because there were so many other cases, other claims, and the day had long since ended and one wanted to get home.

This was a dangerous and unfair attitude I tried hard to resist, but one that the sheer volume of petitions would sometimes force upon me. It was dangerous in the sense that one of these seemingly discardable criminal petitions might carry within it the seed of an important constitutional right. Such a case was that of Clarence Earl Gideon, a woebegone from the Florida panhandle, whose dogged requests for a lawyer resulted in one of the most celebrated Supreme Court rulings of the century, that establishing the right of an indigent state felony defendant to have counsel represent him at trial.[9] Another case, less well known but in its own way just as remarkable, was that of Leon Chambers, fifty-two, black, father of nine, a construction worker in the tiny farm town of Woodville, Mississippi.[10]

Woodville has been described by one writer as "a two-saw-mill, one-cotton-gin town of 1,600, south of Natchez, near the Louisiana border, an area steeped in poverty, illiteracy, and segregation."[11] It is the boyhood home of Jefferson Davis, the birthplace of two Confederate generals, and was pictured by the Wilkinson County Civil War Centennial Committee as "the town most typical of the old South, least changed in appearance and tradition." The town's last movie theatre, The Joy, stands deserted, a block from the courthouse square; it was closed about five years ago to avoid admitting blacks. Whites in Woodville and Wilkinson County have also abandoned the public school system, which is now all black, for a private academy.

On a hot Saturday evening, June 14, 1969, two Woodville policemen, James Foreman and Aaron Liberty, confronted an angry crowd of some fifty or sixty blacks in front of Hay's Café and Pool Hall while trying to make an arrest.[12] Foreman radioed for assistance, and three deputy sheriffs arrived. Once more the officers attempted the arrest but were again repulsed by the crowd. During this commotion, Liberty, himself a black, was shot four times in the back. Before dying Liberty turned and discharged both barrels of his shotgun into an alley from whence his assailant's shots appeared to come. Liberty's first shot went high and scattered the crowd at the face of the alley, but his second shot struck a man running down the alley in the back of the head. That man was Leon Chambers.

Chambers, initially left for dead, survived and was brought to trial for Liberty's murder. From the beginning, however, he professed innocence. His trial revealed baffling, quite contradictory testimony. One deputy sheriff swore he was standing several feet from Liberty and saw Chambers shoot him; another said he saw Chambers "break his arm down" shortly before the shots were fired. A defense witness, however, stated he had been looking at Chambers when the shooting began and was sure Chambers did not fire the shots. Yet two more witnesses testified that one Gable McDonald, not Chambers, had killed Liberty. A sworn out-of-court confession by McDonald to Chambers' attorneys was even introduced, but McDonald repudiated the confession, saying he had given it only on promise of a sizable reward. In the end the all-white jury convicted Chambers of first-degree murder, with life imprisonment. The Mississippi Supreme Court affirmed the verdict.

At this point, Chambers and his case might have passed into oblivion but for one problem: the jury that convicted Leon Chambers had listened to only a half-told story. McDonald had on three separate occasions and to three different individuals confessed to Liberty's murder. At trial, however, the Court refused to allow these individuals even to tell of McDonald's confession on the grounds that such testimony would be hearsay. Chambers' lawyers were further prevented from challenging McDonald's repudiation of his sworn confession by another Mississippi rule of evidence preventing a party from impeaching his own witness (the defense had called McDonald to the stand when the State refused). Thus Chambers' predicament was clear. He had wanted to bring before the jury testimony establishing his claim of innocence, testimony that Mississippi rules of evidence would not allow.

But Chambers pressed his claim beyond Mississippi to the United States Supreme Court, which granted certiorari. And at argument before the Court, Chambers' attorney, Peter Westen, pressed the Justices with the simple equity of Chambers' claim: "The petitioner, Leon Chambers, was convicted of a murder which another man was seen committing and to which the other man spontaneously and repeatedly confessed on the night of the shooting."[13] The appeal was successful. In an opinion written by Justice Powell and joined by seven other Justices, the Court concluded that Chambers had not received a fair trial, "that the exclusion of this critical evidence, coupled with the State's refusal to permit Chambers to cross-examine McDonald, denied him a trial in accord with traditional and fundamental standards of due process."[14] The *Criminal Law Reporter* interpreted the *Chambers* decision as a constitutional landmark, noting that "two widely approved common-law rules of evidence are thrown into serious question by the U.S. Supreme Court as it holds that they were unconstitutionally applied against a Mississippi murder defendant in a case characterized by weak prosecution facts and by strong defense testimony that was kept from the jury."[15] As to Leon Chambers, the State could now dismiss charges or request a new trial, but this time one with the relevant evidence admitted.

When reading a case like *Chambers* v. *Mississippi* I used to wonder what the protagonist, a man like Chambers, was thinking, and if his life had somehow been touched or altered by being the center of an important case in the United States Supreme Court. A visitor to Woodville in 1972, over three years after Liberty's death and shortly before the Supreme Court handed down its decision, found that Chambers' "health is broken and his hearing is ruined by wounds from the shooting."[16] But his faith in his innocence and in the outcome appeared resolute: "I think they're gonna let me go because Mr. Clark and Mr. Westen turned in a good report to the Supreme Court."[17] It fascinated me how this claim of a soft-spoken black man from a Mississippi farm town somehow overcame the local forces against it and worked its way, against all odds, up to the United States Supreme Court, there to leave a wake far beyond Chambers' individual case.

But how would Chambers react? Would he think that to reach and win at the United States Supreme Court the stars had to have been shining in his favor, that something had happened far larger than himself, or would he treat the whole thing in a matter-of-fact kind of way, happy something came along that might help him to get himself off?

There are many Leon Chamberses and Clarence Earl Gideons who come before the Supreme Court. The subjects of its cases seem to be so often society's unfortunates seeking a better shake. Many of Justice Powell's early opinions involved such persons: Willie Mae Weber, requesting workmen's compensation benefits for her illegitimate children;[18] Demetrio Rodriguez, seeking more state funds for the public schools of poor, largely Mexican-American Edgewood School district, where his three young sons attended;[19] David Strange, a one-time criminal defendant from whom the State of Kansas sought repayment for the cost of providing him counsel at trial;[20] Fre Le Poole Griffiths, a Belgian alien who asked the right to practice law in Connecticut;[21] and, of course, Leon Chambers.

The disadvantaged do not always win, for the arguments against them are both formidable and persuasive. But working at the Supreme Court afforded me a glimpse into that other America of prisons and poverty and prejudice, where the American dream has largely ceased to exist, save perhaps in some dim and often disappointed hope. Yet it is society's unfortunates and unconventionals who give a Constitution its mettle, for the broad, middle segment of our nation does not often face censorship of its speech, official

invasion of its homes, or that particular genus of dep-
rivation and prejudice demanding vindication of constitutional rights.

Often I marveled that the job of vindicating the
dispossessed in our system fell so frequently to Justices of the Supreme Court, themselves most frequently possessed of the very best American society
and education has to offer. But the combination
seemed generally to have worked: what we hail as
great advances in national justice may represent a
curious convergence of the most patrician and educated figures in American society with some of the
most forlorn.

Supreme Court cases impart a remarkable education to those who care to read them, an in-depth focus
on a single individual or locality whose predicament is
more often than not reflective of some broader problem. The focus on a particular case may give a truer
reflection of the problem than the more polemical
statements so often found in public discourse. A record of the history and local stratagems in a school
desegregation suit before the Supreme Court, for example, provides an entirely different illumination on
America's race problem than the more general con-
demnations and defenses of racism offered up in political debate.

In politics, the tendency is to start with general public attitudes that are then negotiated and broken down
into particular and, one hopes, workable legislation.
In the courts, this process is reversed and particular
facts are digested and analyzed for what they may yield
in the way of more general truths. For me, research
into a case meant not only an education in the particu-

lar problem involved but, somewhat less consciously, into the nature of the judicial process as well. I came to feel that separation of powers meant not only the check and balance of *power* among the different branches, but the check of one kind of *process* on another, an intricately conceived play-off between legislature and judiciary of two entirely different approaches to many common national problems.

However instructive clerking on the Supreme Court was regarding the workings of an important part of American government, its primary value to me was as a prospective lawyer. Clerking is for most a one- or two-year interlude between law school and law practice or teaching, but an interlude that may prove invaluable to a later career. As a clerk, reading hundreds of briefs and certiorari petitions, I was able to see first-hand the efforts of a broad cross-section of the country's attorneys. The notion sometimes arises that only the best foot of the legal profession is put forward in the Supreme Court. Nothing could be less true. It is the litigants, not the Supreme Court, who for the most part control the lawyers who come before it, and their arguments range from the most refined and skilled to something that would scarcely grace a busy day in traffic court.

The Supreme Court, like any other, must rely upon the efforts of the attorneys in a case. How well the Court ultimately performs will depend to a considerable extent upon how lawyers perform before it. I always hoped that counsel, recognizing the importance of litigation before the Court as well as the Court's substantial burdens, would submit focused, well-structured and researched briefs. A great many did. Yet I also researched cases for Justice Powell where the briefs were scanty, relevant precedents had been ignored, supporting data omitted, and the hard and critical questions avoided. This could be a difficult chore that bogged down planning and operation in our chambers and crowded consideration of other, equally important cases.

Frustrating to me as a clerk were lawyers who took forever to come to the point, lawyers whose submissions began with an exhaustive history of the case, lengthy bows to notions of due process, wholesale and indiscriminate quotations from prior Supreme Court decisions, like some baseball hurler in an elaborate windup who never delivers the pitch. Another aggravation in petitions for certiorari was the "shotgun technique," where counsel, often with not a single significant question to raise, would throw in six or seven frivolous ones. I felt that this was not only an abuse of the judicial process but a disservice to the client as well.

Among the most successful litigants before the Supreme Court is the federal government, whose submissions to the Court—both briefs and certiorari requests—are drafted or monitored by the Solicitor General's office. The government may enjoy a formidable advantage over opponents, not necessarily because of the interests it represents, but because it petitions the Supreme Court in clear, straightforward terms, informs it at the outset why a case is or is not significant, gives an orderly and concise rendition of the facts and the most potent and direct arguments for its position. A meandering, turgid private effort matched against an easily digested government brief, in a Court with a great many matters to consider, may, for the private party, spell outright disaster.

For a case the Supreme Court has decided to hear, written briefs are but one part of counsel's contribution. The other is oral argument by counsel to the Court, in many ways the most dramatic and challenging part of the appellate process. I was once told, by someone who ought to have known better, that oral argument at the Court was of secondary importance to the briefs, little more than a formality for Justices "who have already decided what they're going to do." His view was sadly unfounded: the Justices would hardly devote such time to oral argument—the better part of eight days a month—merely to indulge a pointless exercise.

It was Justice Harlan who best underscored the importance of oral argument in an article written shortly after he came to the Court. "Judges," he said, "have different work habits. There are some judges who listen better than they read and who are more receptive to the spoken than the written word."[22] Unlike the written brief, good oral argument is give-and-take between counsel and bench; a tough, probing exchange can uncover facts or grounds of decision the briefs might obscure and allow a Justice to test on counsel his misgivings and concerns about a case. From counsel's point of view, oral argument is his only chance to address the Justices collectively and face-to-face. They become for one hour a captive audience to every case, and the opportunity for persuasion can be choice.

It is on days of oral argument that the Supreme Court is most alive. The small first-floor cafeteria becomes a hub of activity, with its swarms of tourists and dark-suited lawyers huddling intently at their tables. Members of the press, perhaps John MacKenzie, of the *Washington Post,* or Fred Graham, formerly of *The New York Times* and now with CBS, might stroll through. Occasionally, Solicitor General Griswold would appear, bedecked in formal tux and tails. Eating breakfast there, I would sometimes be interrupted by friends dropping by and wanting to know what seats in the courtroom were available that day.

The courtroom itself, where argument takes place, is elegant in its simplicity. It is of clean, rectangular composition, somewhat higher than it is wide, and ringed about with twenty-four columns of Italian marble. It is imposing but at the same time sufficiently intimate to give dialogue between counsel and Court a conversational tone, not one of formal debate. Institutions of government, even in a democracy, require an aura of drama and ceremony, and the Supreme Court, on a day of argument, is no exception. The courtroom is a theatrical creation, with its high, ornate ceiling, its bench of rich, deep mahogany behind which are the high-backed black leather chairs of the Justices and the red velvet curtain from which they emerge, black-robed, promptly at 10:00 A.M., as the marshal bangs his gavel and announces solemnly,

The Honorable, the Chief Justice, and the Associate Justices of the Supreme Court of the United States. Oyez! Oyez! Oyez! All persons having business before the Honorable, the Supreme Court of the United States, are admonished to draw near and give their attention, for the Court is now sitting. God save the United States and this Honorable Court.

Again the gavel falls, the Justices and all others take their seats, and the day's business begins.

The spotlight at oral argument is on counsel and the Court. The clerks sit in an alcove on the south side of the courtroom, a forgotten part of the whole proceeding. As a clerk, I was generally kept too busy to observe more than a fraction of the cases argued. When I did listen, I witnessed counsel of all ages and skills, from the youngest to the most prestigious elder statesmen of the bar, from the most urbane lawyers to the most roughhewn.

Argument at its best is an illuminating and rapid-paced exercise, at its worst pedantic and unprofitable, sending spectators and judges alike into bouts of drowsiness. Argument before the Court can also take a most unpredictable bent, such as when one celebrated lawyer, after several evasions, finally answered, "I don't know, your honor," to a question on a critical fact of his case; or when an Assistant Attorney General from a Midwestern state failed to cite, when asked, a single federal precedent for his position; or, more pleasantly, when a young, green-looking attorney still in his twenties gave a plucky argument in the face of stiff questioning by the Justices in a significant search and seizure case.

I never sat long in that courtroom, however, without recognizing that effective oral argument before the Supreme Court of the United States demands the very best from a lawyer. Personally, he has to communicate candor and directness, confidence but not arrogance, and, in the case of the great advocates, an appropriate touch of humor and eloquence. Intellectually, he needs a determined instinct for the jugular of his case, and the agility of mind to take advantage of play as it develops, to synchronize the questions of the Justices with the logic and momentum of his own argument. Model appellate advocates are exceedingly rare; when one does perform, it is a thing of exquisite grace and power, a view of a master artist at work.

Clerking on the Supreme Court afforded me not only an excellent view of the nation's legal profession, but a panorama of the American court system as well. The great majority of cases that reach the Supreme Court have undergone extensive rounds of litigation in the lower federal and state courts. It is in those courts that a case is molded and cast, its essential facts found, its record developed, and the initial legal determinations made. By the time it reaches the Supreme Court, a lawsuit is well into adulthood; if it has been sloppily nurtured by the lower courts, the Supreme Court is considerably disadvantaged in its own dealings with it.

Yet the job of the lower courts is much more extensive and important than merely grooming a case for the Supreme Court. Less than 1 percent of all litigation ever reaches the Court, and in the other 99 percent the word of the lower courts is final. Even where the Supreme Court does rule, more questions may be raised than resolved. The Court's most famous twentieth-century decision, *Brown* v. *Board of Education*,[23] held that a state could not maintain a segregated school system. But exactly what constituted a segregated system and how a once-segregated school district must go about achieving dual or integrated status was not really addressed by the Supreme Court for almost another fifteen years.[24] In the interim the lower federal courts struggled mightily with such questions, and their rulings on the difficult and delicate problems of school and race were the law of the land. Even had the Supreme Court addressed these problems during the fifteen-year span, more questions for the lower courts would have remained. For no case is ever entirely controlled by another; each is unique on its facts; distinctions can and often should be made. The Supreme Court may be a judicial ruler, but it is one whose edicts are constantly in need of fresh interpretation. And I was struck by how easily our whole system might be undermined from within if the interpretations were not faithfully and skillfully made.

I have been hesitant to agree when someone once implied in conversation with me that clerking for the Supreme Court must be akin to a year's admission to Mount Olympus. It might be, of course, in the sense that the Supreme Court is the pinnacle of the American legal system, and clerking there affords a dramatic overview of thousands of lawyers and judges at work. Yet I left there feeling that the Court, for all its awesome power, is a curiously dependent institution— perhaps our most dependent branch of government. Since it is a Court, and can only act when a particular case comes before it, it must rely in a quite substantial way on litigants and their lawyers, lower courts, and legal scholarship. For the Court is not just an institution of government but a representative of a profession, with whose style and skills it operates, and on which it depends mightily for the quality of its governing role. Its place in that profession seemed to me much like that of a queen on a chess board, sweeping and devastating in its own inherent powers, but, over the long run, ineffectual unless moving in concert and cooperation with the other pieces.

In another, more personal sense the image of the Supreme Court as Mount Olympus was plainly wrong. The atmosphere at the Court is not cold or formidable but relaxed and sometimes rather intimate. Talking with friends who worked at the Pentagon, the State Department, or the Department of Health, Education and Welfare, I sensed a contrast analogous to that between an Alpine village and Manhattan Island. For unlike those other governmental leviathans, the Supreme Court has a relatively small staff—around three hundred full-time employees—the sum of whom are able to park underneath the building or in a small lot around back, and most of whom know one another. The staff at the Court is extraordinarily friendly and helpful, even to one-year squatters such as law clerks, and the day would often go down more easily after talking with one of the security guards about his weekend fishing trip or bantering with Lula Allen, the "All right, keep it moving, now" personality at the Supreme Court cafeteria, or chattering somewhat more quietly with Edward Hudon, the Court librarian, about his legal writings and experience or with Mike Rodak, the knowledgeable and gregarious chief clerk.

The warmth at the Court came to me in quite different ways, perhaps as a greeting in a corridor or elevator, or through listening to Justice Stewart late one afternoon talk of his days as a Cincinnati City Councilman, or by seeing Justice Rehnquist, leading the carolers to the piano accompaniment of his law clerk, at the Court's annual Christmas party. One afternoon the Court's barber, who had worked there many years, regaled me with stories of Justices whose hair he had cut. His reminiscing ended with an affectionate tribute to Justice Frankfurter. "That man," he said, "would come sit in this chair like he knew all there was to know about law." I could see that that barber and others like him were important to the Court. The Justices, under the pressure and deadlines of difficult decisions, naturally worked most effectively against a backdrop of friendliness and cordiality.

There were points of relief in a day of clerking to which I looked forward with great relish. One was lunch, where clerks from the various chambers would generally get together. We were provided a small and separate dining room—several long tables pushed together—in which no outsiders, not even spouses, were normally permitted. Occasionally, there was an invited guest, Senators Phil Hart and Edward Kennedy, acting FBI director Patrick Gray, Solicitor General Erwin Griswold, and Dan Rather of CBS News were among those I remember. Each of the Justices also ate with us once a term, and took questions afterward on an informal and confidential basis. Mostly, however, it was just clerks, and conversation flowed freely, a mixture of shop talk with lots of very warm air about politics, sports, and other handy topics. Lunches were useful to throw out ideas on the law to a very critical audience and for general talk about the Court. Lunches were also the time when the Justices were away, often in their own dining room, and a passing irreverence would seize us, inspiring remarks on how the Court "really fouled up" such and such case, and so on.

Lunch hour provided the best opportunities to come to know one's fellow clerks. Occasionally, I would read of Supreme Court law clerks as being "bright young men," from "leading law schools," on "the first step to a very promising career." The following description is rather typical:

> A Supreme Court clerkship, which is sought after by the highest ranking law school graduates each year, usually comes as a capstone to a brilliant law school career. And a clerkship often leads to a distinguished career in private practice, in teaching or in government service.[25]

A respected former law clerk to Justice Frankfurter is quoted as saying, "A list of Supreme Court clerks reads like the 'Who's Who' of the American legal profession. These guys are your law school all-Americans."[26]

Such depictions are, of course, flattering, but they struck me much in the same way as pictures of well-scrubbed, artificially wholesome students who often adorn the covers of college catalogues. The clerks I knew did not generally regard themselves as some ordained group; most, in fact, acknowledged the large element of breaks and good fortune that led to their appointments. They were, of course, able lawyers, and I acquired over time genuine intellectual respect for fellow Powell clerks with whom I had the chance to work closely. One was as supple in handling abstract concepts as any lawyer I had met, and another an excellent researcher and writer with a marvelous command of Court precedent. But there were other graduating law students who might have brought their special talents to the job and pleased Justice Powell as well as, if not better than, we did. There seems to me to be an inevitable unfairness in any attempt at prestige labeling, and that of the Supreme Court clerkship is no exception.

The gratification of clerking lay in personal as well as intellectual relationships with fellow clerks, most of whom were determined to enjoy life as well as to succeed in it. My friends among the clerks felt the need for a life outside the law. Tennis, bicycling, and hiking were popular activities, as were such handicrafts as weaving or pottery. One clerk explained to me that after working with legal abstractions all day, "I find it enormously therapeutic just to do something concrete with my hands."

But the greatest of all clerking sidelines was basketball, which eight or ten of us played about twice a week late in the afternoon in the Court's small gymnasium. (One bad joke that continues to be told is that the basketball floor, located on the third story, directly above the courtroom, is truly the highest "court" in the world.) Our games were not unlike any pickup match at a public park, a melee of free-verse talent and clumsiness, known in the vernacular as jungle ball. We refereed our own struggles, played under a loose and shifting set of rules, and in "uniforms" of different colors, shapes, sizes, and states of cleanliness. Once every so often an "All-Star" team of clerks challenged the Court's police force or the night maintenance crew, with mixed success. Occasionally, too, Justice

White would participate; he is a talented hoopster who once demolished me in a game of "horse" with a series of left-handed set and hook shots. Justice White also plays aggressively and very competitively. Going after a loose ball one game, he and I collided: the Justice stood firm while I skidded across the floor and into a wall. No one called Foul.

Relationships between Justices and clerks are generally cordial, and the Supreme Court is remarkable in the extent to which it takes law clerks into its trust. One proceeding to which no clerk has ever been admitted, however, is the conference, which is reserved exclusively to the Justices themselves. Conference may be the Supreme Court's most dramatic hour, for it is there that the Justices, alone among themselves, first discuss and vote on cases before the Court and significant petitions for certiorari.

It is essential to the orderly functioning of the Supreme Court that discussion among the Justices at conference remain inviolate. For conference decisions, important as they are, are only tentative; both votes and grounds for decision may switch upon the subsequent circulation of written opinion drafts. The entire process at the Supreme Court, in fact, points inexorably to but one ultimate product: the written opinion, generally announced by its author from the Supreme Court bench on Monday mornings. The opinion represents the Court's final and official act in a case, the only thing of all the Court's study and deliberation that is ever made public, and ultimately all of a case that endures. However effortless or unanimous in appearance, the Court's opinion may have meant hours of intense discussion, negotiation, and compromise among the Justices. Such preliminary discussion, including the important exchanges among the Justices at conference, must be frank and uninhibited by the fear that something might later be made public to confuse or lessen the integrity of the final written product on which the Court has come to rest.

The conference normally is held on Friday, though when the agenda is crowded, some discussion may be scheduled earlier in the week. Though no outsider attends them, several of the Justices have described how typical conferences proceed:[27]

The Justices arrive promptly at 10:00 A.M., and by long tradition each Justice shakes hands with those already present. The custom apparently was started by Chief Justice Melville Fuller, as a symbol that "harmony of aims if not of views is the Court's guiding principle,"[28] and a reminder at the outset that personal respect can transcend the sharp divergence of judicial judgments.

The conference room itself is oak paneled, and over the mantel facing the large, rectangular mahogany conference table is a portrait of Chief Justice John Marshall. On the back of each black leather chair is a metal plate bearing a Justice's name. At one end of the table sits Chief Justice Burger with the Associate Justices along the sides. The Justices' carts with their relevant notes and memoranda surround the table. The Court's sole link with the outside world is the junior Justice, William Rehnquist, who jars the door slightly to give or receive a message.

The Chief Justice runs the conference. His is recognized as a difficult job, requiring a sense of pace, of knowing when to curtail a drifting discussion or to call a break. The Chief must also keep straight the various items up for consideration and begin discussion of each case with a short synopsis and a summary of his own views. Discussion then proceeds in order of seniority, from Justice William O. Douglas, the senior Associate, through to Justice Rehnquist, the Court's most recent appointee. As the Court may have as many as fifty to seventy-five cases, petitions, motions, and administrative matters on a day's agenda, the time each Justice speaks on each item is normally quite brief, perhaps no more than a half minute on the normal petition for certiorari. (This limited time may have prompted Justice James McReynolds to note that an "overspeaking judge is no well-tuned cymbal.")[29] In cases that have been argued before the Court during the week, where much more extended discussion occurs than on the normal petition for certiorari, each Justice may act as his own secretary, taking notes for later reference as his colleagues explain their positions.

If the Supreme Court is to function smoothly, the utmost sensitivity and courtesy is required from each Justice toward his brethren, an important form of judicial self-restraint not often mentioned in discourses on the subject. The operating premise of the Court is that the deep-seated judicial differences among the Justices not be allowed to boil over into personal animosities, a premise that the Court to a remarkable extent observes. Justice Powell would often return from the end of a day-long conference debate on the most complicated and controversial cases, commenting how through it all a sense of decorum and personal consideration prevailed. Occasionally, however, heated moments do arise. Justice Tom Clark tells the story of a conference many terms back when the first Justice John M. Harlan and Justice Oliver Wendell Holmes served on the Court. "Harlan was presenting his view of a case with which Holmes evidently did not agree. In the midst of Harlan's argument, Holmes interrupted with the sharp remark, 'That won't wash! That won't wash!' . . . Fortunately, the Chief Justice at the time was Melville Fuller. He had already discussed the case and his position was similar to that of Harlan. When the diminutive, but courageous, silver-haired, handlebar-mustached Chief Justice realized that all was not well between his brothers he quickly answered Holmes' 'That won't wash' with a cheery 'Well, I'm scrubbing away, anyhow.' A tense situation passed over during the ensuing laughter."[30]

Though as law clerks we did not, of course, attend the conferences, we did help prepare for them. Friday mornings could be busy, as we thought of last-minute matters to mention to the Justice or worked with Sally and Spencer to make sure memoranda, cert notes, motions, or whatever were in the Justice's notebooks and in the proper order. I was relieved when, shortly before ten, Spencer's cart finally clattered down the marble corridor to the conference room. Late in the afternoon, sometime between four and half-past five, conference would adjourn, and the Justice might come back and tell us how the day went. Justice Powell had pursued a rigorous schedule all his working life, but after the concentration of an extended conference, he would be tired and quite drained. Still, he would arrive with an unmistakable broad grin when he had news he knew you would like to hear. "Larry, you might be interested in what happened" in such and such a case, and he would say what the vote was. I remember one day being quite disappointed in the way a particular case had turned out, and the disappointment must have shown on my face. "Sorry, Jay," he said, with something of a wink at my fellow clerks. "You were just on the wrong side of the generation gap in that one."

The Friday conference ended the Court's official week, but its work week continued. Many Justices and clerks found in weekends an indispensable stretch of uninterrupted time in which to complete some pressing task. Occasionally, I would be asked by someone interested in the Supreme Court's schedule how long and hard I, as a law clerk, worked. The question, of course, is not so serious as when asked of a Justice. The workload on clerks does not have the cumulative wear that it might on a Justice. Clerks, furthermore, do not bear the responsibility of final decision, and it is less critical that they have time for reflection. Then, too, no graduating law student would shy away from the experience of a Supreme Court clerkship, no matter what the demands of the job. Still, clerks on the Supreme Court are and have to be a hard-working lot. During the term, I worked six full days a week and three evenings, which I guess was about average. Even so, I may have been better off than many of my predecessors, who worked in the days when Justices had only one or two clerks. Once when I mentioned to Spencer Campbell that clerking seemed a tough job, he told me that Justice Black had worked day and night, often as a lone dissenter, "with only one law clerk, Buddy Cooper, all his first three years on the bench." He didn't get any real relief, Spencer stated, until Justice Douglas came on and helped with the dissents. "Just him and that one law clerk, for three years," Spencer said. He smiled and shook his head as if to say I had it easy.

Part of my job as clerk was an attempt to stay on top of detail and paperwork. *Time Magazine* once ran a cartoon showing the Justices of the Supreme Court thrashing and choking in a sea of paperwork,[31] something that evoked an appreciative chuckle from employees at the Court. The Clerk's office, under the direction of Michael Rodak, does an admirable job processing the Court's papers and the submissions of its litigants, and the Court itself is revising its procedures to better cope with the problem. But the number of items, with their sheer volume of paper, that pass through the Supreme Court each term is enormous. As a starter, the Court now handles in a term some 3,600 petitions for certiorari and appeals, each of which, no matter how frivolous, requires in most chambers at least the brief attention of a clerk and a Justice. Then there are various and sundry motions, applications to stay decisions of lower courts, petitions of criminal defendants seeking bail, none of which in and of itself is overwhelming but which collectively peck further away at a Justice's time. Finally, there are the argued cases, decision on which alone would constitute an impressive year's work for the Court.

Each case argued before the Court is in a constant state of evolution, and in the manner of a snowball rolling downhill, each day accumulates unto itself more papers and material: first the briefs of the parties, then the reply, supplementary and amicus briefs and motions, next—after argument and conference—the written opinion drafts, next the concurring and dissenting opinions, then notes from other Justices joining or commenting upon these various opinions, until at last the case is handed down. This process is not intimidating in any one case, but the Court hands down not one, but a bit over a hundred cases with signed opinions each term. During the term, especially from December until late May, the Supreme Court may become something of a marathon, with seventy or so cases alive at any one time and in varying stages of progress, all the way from those scheduled for an upcoming argument to those decided and ready to be handed down. The job of simultaneously keeping abreast of so many items is challenging enough for a clerk, though in our chambers at least, Justice Powell preferred all cases to be divided among us, with one law clerk primarily responsible to him on a third of them. For the Justice himself, with a final responsibility for every matter before the Court, keeping current with developments obviously was a demanding task.

The volume of business before the Supreme Court does not mean that it is choked to the point of paralysis. Justices are able to deal quickly with matters of relatively little importance and with those where they have acquired a background or expertise. What the volume does mean, however, is that much of the work on the Supreme Court is of the "stop-and-go" variety, and that sustained and uninterrupted periods of time for a single difficult problem or opinion are often hard to come by. As a clerk, I found the chances of interruption during any half hour to be impressive, and I seldom returned to my desk without some new matter demanding attention. I was grateful to be able to block off an entire day to do the quality of research Justice Powell wanted and that a complex case required. Some commentators on the Court's work interpret a particular case or opinion as if the Justice who authored it had nothing to do the whole year but sit back and ponder that single problem. But at times the Court's term might more accurately call to mind the proverbial small boy with his spinning tops, running to keep them all going.

The pace and workload at the Supreme Court has increasingly disturbed those who see the need there for a more reflective atmosphere, who understand the vast importance of the Court's judgments, the human limitations of its personnel, and the philosophic element of its decisions. But the Supreme Court is also a branch of modern government upon which are constantly thrust many of the nation's most complex and burning problems and where a keen activity and bustle seem almost necessary if it is not to be left cold or in the lurch. The Court, in fact, is a place of diverse mood, whose most harassed and feverish moments are yet framed by a more profound character.

This character often came through to me in the hours of early evening, when the Court seemed strangely and gratefully quieted. The public had long since departed—the trampling troop of girl scouts and that beleaguered teacher yelling about Justice Holmes to her twitching third-grade class. No more the messengers with stacks of circulating papers, or law clerks bursting in on one another with the newest way to handle a case. The operators had deserted their elevators; even the typewriters and telephones were still.

Perhaps I would spot a lone security guard or a night maintenance man slowly pushing his mop along the floor. But mostly one big, darkened, empty Court. The high ceilings, the marble columns and corridors, the dimly lit busts, gave the Court at this hour an almost religious holiness, the hush of a temple, but a temple to which the most downtrodden and reviled of our countrymen come for grace. The alien and the illegitimate, the racially oppressed, criminally convicted, educationally deprived, politically rejected— all these seek sanctuary in this Court, before these nine priests, who oftentimes take them in.

Clerking at the Supreme Court is being a small part of something much larger than oneself, a minute thread in the grand tradition of the Court and also of several subtraditions, one of which is clerking itself. The tradition of Supreme Court law clerks began in 1882 with Justice Horace Gray, who continued his practice as Chief Justice of the Massachusetts Supreme Court of hiring for one-year terms recent top graduates from Harvard Law School. As public funds were not then available for such legal assistance, Justice Gray paid his law clerk's salary from his own resources. Congress first provided one clerk for each Justice in 1886 at an annual salary of $1,600. Most Justices did not begin to hire a second law clerk until 1947, and a third until the 1970 term, in response to the Court's increasing case burdens.

Nor did law clerks always work for one year and for one Justice, as they do now. Justice Joseph McKenna kept his first clerk for twelve years and had only two other clerks during his remaining fifteen years on the Court. And there was one law clerk who actually served with four Justices, starting with Justice Rufus Peckham in 1905 and ending with Justice George Sutherland in 1924. It was not unusual for the late-nineteenth-century Justices to employ, as clerks, the sons of their colleagues on the Court. Justice William Day and the first John M. Harlan even had their own sons as law clerks. A few interesting stories have survived the early days of law clerking. At least one Justice, James McReynolds, is reported to have been "plagued with troubles in locating and retaining clerks. Especially in his earlier years, he insisted that his clerks remain single and refrain from the use of tobacco."[32]

The tradition of clerking is not a formal one; there are no great public convocations of former Supreme Court law clerks, no newsletter or dues requests from any national association. It is a much more subtle thing, and it took me some time to grow into. A former clerk once told me that accepting the position of Supreme Court law clerk "is like assuming the trademark of some old, respected silversmith; a quality job is expected." Many times, that year at the Court, the goad to an additional hour's work was the determination that the trademark not be besmirched.

In the gallery of public notables are former Supreme Court clerks: the late Secretary of State Dean Acheson was once a clerk to Justice Louis Brandeis, and the former Attorney General Elliot Richardson clerked for Justice Felix Frankfurter. Two Justices of the present Court, Court Byron White and William Rehnquist, clerked for Chief Justice Frederick Vinson and Justice Robert Jackson respectively. Many former clerks have sought some form of professional distinction, either in the practice or teaching of law, often quite a different thing from public recognition. The most gratifying part of clerking, however, really does not lie in the relationship of the clerkship to subsequent attainment.

Though the experience lasts only a year, leaving the Justice for whom one clerked is much like another college graduation: to speak of someone as once a Harlan clerk or a Warren clerk, for example, is almost as if speaking of an alma mater. Once I was rather humorously warned by a professor in law school of a subtle sense of snobbery among former Frankfurter clerks, "something more refined even than that existing among Harvard law graduates at large." The remark may have made great gossip and poor fact, but it is not far-fetched to think that those who have clerked for a Justice share some common collegial bond. Reunions even take place between Justices and former clerks, often on an annual basis, though some are overlaid with a special meaning or poignancy, as when Justice Stewart's clerks presented him with a new judicial robe after fifteen years on the Supreme Court bench or when the clerks of Justice Black gathered at his home for his eighty-fifth-birthday celebration.

Occasionally, a former clerk becomes something of a disciple of the Justice for whom he once worked, a knowledgeable and sympathetic interpreter of the Justice's views and positions to the world outside. Philip Kurland, clerk to Justice Frankfurter in 1945–46, has written often of the late Justice, the most recent contribution being *Mr. Justice Frankfurter and the Constitution*, a distillation of essential Frankfurter for nonlegal scholars. Among the best illuminations into the mind and work habits of Justice Brandeis is provided in an article by Paul Freund, a clerk to the Justice during the 1932 term.[33] In 1969, the seventieth birthday of Justice Harlan and the fifteenth anniversary of his nomination to the Court, David Shapiro, a clerk to the Justice during the 1962 term, edited a vintage collection of Harlan opinions.[34] Charles Reich, before authoring *The Greening of America,* wrote for the *Harvard Law Review* what is often thought a classic interpretation of his former boss, entitled *Mr. Justice Black and the Living Constitution.*[35]

Describing a clerk's attachment to his Justice may leave too parochial an impression. Gradually, I sensed from those who had clerked there a broader allegiance to the Supreme Court as an institution. This did not necessarily mean that they agreed with its particular decisions or with the general direction the Court might pursue. Some of the most trenchant attacks on the Court's direction and the quality of its work have come, in fact, from former clerks.[36] Yet even their most deeply felt opposition seemed encompassed by some larger respect, perhaps the notion that in a democracy there still is genuine need for something like the Supreme Court, that it ought to function in a climate of greater public understanding, that its place must not be degraded by substandard appointments of whatever ideological bent, and that it should strive to be a force of conscientious reason in our national life. Such respect, even in so general a form, is important. Acceptance of a Supreme Court has not always come easily to Americans, and its role needs periodic refurbishing in the face of some most recent unpopular act. The respect of former clerks, speaking and writing frequently about the Supreme Court as many do, may have helped somewhat with the process.

An interesting example of the role of former law clerks surfaced when the so-called Freund Committee was established. The committee was charged by Chief Justice Warren Burger to study the case load at the Supreme Court and recommend such solutions as its findings warranted. Three of the committee's seven members were former Supreme Court law clerks, including Chairman Freund. The committee's main and apparently unanimous recommendation was the creation of a National Court of Appeals to help the Supreme Court screen certiorari petitions and resolve certain of the more minor conflicts among the federal circuit courts of appeal.[37] Almost before this recommendation was officially released, a stiff opposition gathered, much of it from former Supreme Court law clerks. The ensuing debate, with former clerks manning both sides, was carried on in various media and included an especially spirited exchange in the *New Republic* between Alexander Bickel, a committee member and former Frankfurter clerk, and Nathan Lewin, a clerk to Justice Harlan during the 1961 term.[38] All the whacking concerned means not ends, however. Professors Freund and Bickel saw the Court's salvation in a more manageable press of business, their opponents, in not having an essential part of its jurisdiction siphoned off from the Court itself.

The traditions of the Supreme Court clerkship, and the relationship of clerk to Court, were something I had not much pondered until well after my selection by Justice Powell. In some measure, I was brought to it by the questions of those applying for a clerkship with the Justice for the year following my own. Frequently, Justice Powell would introduce the applicants he interviewed to us, his present clerks. In talking with them, I was impressed by the deep vein of talent represented in the applicants and by the difficulty of the job of choosing among them.

The choice of clerks is strictly a personal matter with each Justice, and the selection process varies substantially among the Justices. Some Justices have shown a fondness for a particular school or region with which they were once associated. Justices Gray, Holmes, Brandeis, and Frankfurter relied almost exclusively on Harvard for their clerks. Chief Justice Taft took his clerk each year from the Yale Law School on the recommendation of its then Dean, Charles E. Clark. Justice Frank Murphy reportedly favored the University of Michigan Law School; Justice Pierce Butler, Minnesota; Chief Justice Fred Vinson, Northwestern, and Justice Sherman Minton, Indiana. "Appointment on the basis of the judge's geographical background is also commonplace. . . . Justice Douglas has favored appointees from the West Coast, Justice Black more often than not selected southerners as his clerks, and Justice Whittaker selected his clerks from the Midwest."[39]

Justice Powell often said that the selection of his clerks was among the most important decisions he made during a term. He relied on his clerks not only for legal work but for personal compatibility, without which a year together in a small and interdependent chambers might be grim. The problem of selection was invariably an attempt to cull the best from among a wealth of prospects—in many cases over 150 applicants for three positions. At some point in late September or early October Justice Powell began to narrow the field of 150 to those who might be serious contenders. From these, the Justice would ask a smaller number to the Court for a half-hour interview. Of those whom he interviewed he would ultimately select three.

Applying for a Supreme Court clerkship is an informal process. Anyone with a law degree may technically apply, and since there is no standard application form, each candidate simply assembles his own. Many hopefuls apply simultaneously to several Justices. The stronger applicants present high law school grades, experience on their school's law review, perhaps some brief tenure with a good law firm, and a prior clerkship with a state or lower federal judge, most often one on a federal circuit court of appeals. No one of these credentials is absolutely essential or formally required, though almost all clerks have worked on a law review and a substantial majority of present Supreme Court clerks have had some prior clerking experience on a lower court. The difficult task for Justice Powell was to translate the impressive and virtually indistinguishable paper credentials of the top applicants into a decision as to who would actually do the best job. He was fond of remarking that a good lawyer had to be able to do two things—reason and write—and he reviewed recommendations from those who knew the applicant's work well, with special regard to these qualities.

Above and beyond the credentials of a clerk were

what the Justice used to term "the intangibles." He never actually spelled out what this meant, but it was understood from his own style of work and personal values. He obviously wanted a clerk with a sense of integrity and trustworthiness as to the confidences of Court, as well as a sense of personal loyalty, not as a yes man, but as someone who would go the extra mile in a pinch. He sought clerks of unselfish talent; he often referred to his chambers as "our team" and saw its product as the result of hard collective effort. He had no set views, however, on the personal politics of a prospective clerk and, in fact, never expected his clerks to agree with each vote he cast or opinion he wrote. He preferred that his clerks be of different persuasions and stir "crosswinds," as he once put it, through his office.

Shortly after his confirmation to the Court, Justice Powell wondered whether, being Virginian, most of his clerks would come from the South. But in practice, however, he sought the best individual, irrespective of region. Of the first seven clerks he chose, two were from the law school at the University of Virginia, and one each from Harvard, Yale, Texas, Stanford, and the University of Chicago. Late one afternoon he began to recall where certain of his clerks had been raised. "Let's see, you're from Virginia, Jay, and Larry's from New Mexico and west Texas, Pete comes from Alabama, and Phil from over on the eastern shore of Maryland. Isn't it curious how you're all Southerners?" Then, after a moment, he turned to me and we both laughed at his rather expansive claims for his native region.

Selection as a clerk obviously meant the assumption

of important responsibilities—responsibilities some have thought too great. The influence exerted by law clerks on the course and decisions of the United States Supreme Court has been the subject of much serious discussion. It remains one of the institution's most intriguing and least satisfactorily answered questions. To some extent, it must continue so. By Court tradition, clerks are loyal subordinates whose instinctive discretion shields some of the Court's necessarily most private matters. Self-comment on their role has not been infrequent, but clerks have avoided mentioning examples where disclosure would breach an emphatic, though unwritten, trust.

Yet discussion of the clerk's role and influence has persisted. One classic view is that of present Justice Rehnquist in a 1957 article for *U.S. News and World Report,* written not long after he had served as clerk for Justice Robert Jackson.[40] The Court in the middle and late 1950s had not only outlawed state-imposed school segregation but issued a number of decisions deemed protective of suspected Communists and criminal defendants. As a result, it had assumed its seasonal position as the object of public mistrust. The idea circulated that law clerks, in large part honor graduates of Harvard, Yale, Columbia, and other "liberal" intellectual centers of the Northeast, were quietly and insidiously responsible for the "leftward" trend.

In his article, Mr. Rehnquist agreed that law clerks were a capable and conscientious lot, but generally to the "left" of either the nation or the Court. Clerks, he said, were "an intellectually high-spirited group," some of whom "in their youthful exuberance permit their notions to engender a cynical disrespect for the capabilities of anyone, including Justices, who may disagree with them." The majority of the clerks harbored, in his view, an "extreme solicitude for the claims of Communists and other criminal defendants, expansion of federal power at the expense of State power, great sympathy toward any government regulation of business—in short, the political philosophy now espoused by the Court under Chief Justice Earl Warren." Mr. Rehnquist discounted the idea that the liberal viewpoint of clerks significantly influenced the Court's signed opinions, where a Justice himself could carefully examine the issues and make the product very much his own. But the sheer volume of petitions for certiorari forced Justices to rely heavily on clerks' summary memoranda. Here, unfortunately, an unconscious slant did creep in. "And where," concluded Rehnquist, "such bias did have any effect, because of the political outlook of the group of clerks that I knew, its direction would be to the political 'left.' "

Justice Jackson himself once quipped that the "idea of the law clerks' influence gave rise to a lawyer's waggish statement that the Senate no longer need bother about confirmation of Justices but ought to confirm the appointment of law clerks."[41] However facetious, the lawyer's statement betrayed a too frequent misconception about the role of clerks at Court. The entire process of decision at the Supreme Court involves the interplay of a great many factors, of which the input of the law clerks is undoubtedly one. But the subject of law-clerk influence deserves to be appraised realistically, not in the course of seeking a scapegoat for some unpopular set of actions taken by the Supreme Court. Law clerks do indeed have an influence at Court, but one that is often misleadingly inflated.

The obvious and primary truth about the Supreme Court of the United States is that the Justices themselves control it. They are but nine in number, and the responsibility of each is intensely personal. A Justice must discuss each case with his colleagues at conference and in each he must cast a final and public vote. Opinions on the most heated subjects—abortion, school desegregation, capital punishment—bear his name. There are no committees such as in Congress or departments and special advisory groups such as in the executive to which he may shunt matters of particular complexity. A Justice further bears a heavy accountability for his performance, not just in the comments of contemporary critics, but in the larger legal and historical judgment gradually forming on his tenure. Finally, he must square his enormous power to affect the nation's life with the private soundings of his personal conscience. The core responsibilities of this kind of trust are simply nondelegable.

Judging, as its name implies, ought ultimately to be an individual act. Justice Jackson once observed that "a court is one place where counsel should confront and address the very men who are to decide his case. I do not think judging can be a staff job, and I deplore whatever tendency there may be in the courts to make it such."[42] Whatever different kinds of tasks law clerks perform in their respective chambers, it is universally apparent that the Justice retains a close and direct supervision. Any other notion is implausible on its face. A Supreme Court Justice is a man of intelligence, broad life experience, prior public or professional distinction, and with a deeply felt conviction of what is best for the country and the place of judicial power in achieving it. He would not likely hand over the day's affairs to someone freshly out of law school and new to the business of the Court. The best evidence of this is that a Justice's votes and judicial expressions while on the Court remain consistent or in a state of chartable evolution and do not veer haphazardly from year to year with the presence of different law clerks.

Often overlooked are two major institutional safeguards at the Supreme Court that, in fact, make law clerks less puissant and entrenched than many a senior staffer in the legislative or executive branches. Though Justices may enjoy the longest tenure in our government, their legal staff experiences the shortest. Law clerks in the vast majority of cases hold their jobs for no more than one year. This rapid turnover restricts sharply the influence of the clerks. Much of the first part of the year is spent learning the ropes, mastery of which may only shortly precede one's time for departure.

The second safeguard lies simply in the mechanics of decision making at the Supreme Court, which affords the Justice in every important instance a chance to check his clerk's impressions: in significant petitions for certiorari the check is the discussion at conference and in argued cases it is the word of counsel, the conference discussion, and later circulation of written opinions among the Justices themselves. Something of an exception to this rule may exist among the less significant petitions for certiorari, where law clerks, in an effort to handle the volume, may have a Justice's permission to write him an abbreviated memo on a case the clerk thinks patently unimportant. This discretion, however, seems insignificant in the overall scheme of the Court's business. As former Justice Arthur J. Goldberg noted, "An astonishing number of filed cases [petitions for certiorari] raises questions that a third-year law student can immediately recognize as inappropriate for the Supreme Court."[43]

The theory of excessive law clerk influence often rests on a monolithic impression of law clerks themselves, a fear that law clerks as a group are somehow out to "radicalize" the Court. The personal philosophy of the average Supreme Court clerk may, in common parlance, be "liberal" or "left-of-center" if such terms imply a heightened sensitivity to the rights of minorities and the underprivileged, a somewhat greater confidence in federal than in state government, and a more frequent libertarian preference for rights of privacy and free expression over governmental efforts at their control. But such philosophies are hardly very different from those of some Justices. And, as Justices differ, so do their law clerks. Some I knew were of a "conservative" bent, while others were simply uncharacterizable, having perhaps an expansive view of the protections that the First Amendment affords free expression and a more narrow notion of the rights of privacy protected by the Fourth.

The charge of radicalized law clerks is mainly amusing. Alexander Bickel has noted that "only on the hysterical assumption that our universities are staffed by Machiavellian radicals and that our brightest young men are incapable of thinking for themselves can such an assertion be maintained."[44] Law schools in America above all else teach "due process," that is, a commitment to order and proper channeling, to reform of structures from within, to management of the levers and mastery of the intricacies of our system and not to its basic impairment or destruction. Law clerks by and large are exemplary products of the "system," with a strong vested interest in its continuance. To at least the same extent as a lawyer is an original thinker, he is also a technician and craftsman, dedicated to the imperatives of a process and to making it work. For clerks this means pride in the best job possible, even if privately one might disavow the result. It means an eye for accuracy, thoroughness, precedent, and the lines of one's logic, a kind of intuitive and neutral instinct that very often overrides personal ideology. Most lawyers and law clerks in the service of the system find themselves occasionally participating in one cause or another they do not adore; the prime instinct is not to subvert or rebel, but simply to make the best of it.

The idea that law clerks represent some independent force of resistance within the Court or that they somehow thwart or undermine a Justice's personal will is a piece of mythology that ought to be buried. The prevailing spirit between clerk and Justice is one of loyalty and cooperation. The best clerks I knew were those who took a Justice's basic philosophy as a given and tried to work within that framework. The least effective course would be to attempt continually to convince a Justice to take positions that, given his personal philosophy and past decisions, were simply inconceivable. A clerk is a small point on the continuum of the Justice's development, and the trick is to contribute effectively to that development, to synchronize one's own patterns of thought and expression with those of the Justice, in short, to move on his wavelength. One former clerk to Justice Black put it rather well:

> You started out being a little sophomoric in your approach in that you would look at the cases as if you were the justice and make your recommendations. But I found very quickly that I slipped into the posture of understanding how he would vote on the cases and . . . the recommendations that I made tended to conform to what I thought he would do if he had gone through all the same papers that I had just sat down with.[45]

The relationship between Justice and clerk does not relegate the clerk to a mindless, agreeably nodding role. Justice Powell certainly never made us feel this way. Before hearing argument in a case, the Justice might request a fifteen or twenty minute conference with the clerk to whom he had assigned it. He used these meetings in an exploratory fashion, pondering the significance of critical facts, or the implications of a proposed result and how far its logic might tide over to related, hypothetical situations. Often he would want to probe the principles he had set forth in previous opinions and their applicability to the case at hand. Throughout, he used his clerk as a sounding board, in the hope of receiving some feedback and tension that he might use to hone his own ideas. He liked to do some fraction of his thinking out loud and interpersonally, with a second mind to spin and work ideas around.

Sometimes in these discussions I sensed the Justice to be firmly committed in a case, while in others I would leave not knowing exactly how he intended to vote. Once he said to me, "Well, Jay, you've persuaded me on this one," and for a moment, I felt terribly sagacious, until I reflected that I had no more than confirmed a view to which he himself had seemed partial all along. I never entirely understood just how I figured in his reflections, for a clerk's input is but one of many strands in the process of decision at the Court. The genius of that process is that a Justice is virtually compelled to butt against a particular case on at least five or six different occasions before his vote becomes final. He has an initial quick acquaintance with the case when certiorari is granted, followed some months later by his reading of the briefs, then his listening to oral argument, next his discussion of the case with other Justices at conference, perhaps some later, informal discussion with one or more colleagues, and lastly, his writing or reading of the circulated Court opinions and dissents. Sandwiched somewhere amidst these different events may be a discussion with his law clerk. But where and how during this process a Justice makes up his mind in a case was a mystery to me, as perhaps, in certain instances, it is to the Justice himself.

Very seldom as a clerk was there time for detached observance of this process, the pace and demands of the job so enveloped me. I recall often how I felt clerking, day by day, of the loneliness of long Saturday hours in the library, of bruises to my ego when a fellow clerk refuted my logic, of the tedium of a search through the *Congressional Record,* of the frustration when votes and cases went against my hope. But also of the compensating satisfactions—of feeling a subject well thought through and, mainly, of hearing Justice Powell after hours of joint effort finally be satisfied, looking over in a quiet way to say, "O.K., Jay, let her go." At times, I became consumed in such moments, so emotionally drained by minor victories and disappointments that I wondered if the term would ever end.

Clerking was exhausting because it was so engrossing, because it combined so much: the excitement of proximity to enormous power with an intellectual exhilaration and discipline, and often a moral and humanitarian aim. There are seats in a civilization where its deeper spirit seems to reside, where its most elevated discourse may take place, where its ideals are set and much of its history made. The Supreme Court at its best can be such a place; perhaps more than any other, its vindication lies with history. Its lowest hours have been those where it failed to lead or where it set its face against time as in the tragic episode of Dred Scott, the blessing of Jim Crow in *Plessy* v. *Ferguson,* or its ill-starred efforts to slow the New Deal. It is history that gives the dissenter his due, one thinks, looking at the large framed portraits of Holmes and Brandeis on the Court's first floor. Each term the opinions of Court are set forth in thick volumes, whose numbered bindings, 405, 406, 407 . . . link with the past and the hundreds of volumes to come after. "Oyez, oyez, oyez," another day's business will commence; Chief

Justice Burger announces the case, and argument begins. Justice Marshall whispers to Justice Powell; Justice White leans intently forward and questions; Justices Douglas and Blackmun appear deep in thought. The day winds on, and one watches, listens, wondering how this particular present will emerge in hindsight. Their judging is never easy; there are no plain trailmarks to historical favor, no magical way to discern what is evanescent among us and what will or should endure.

When I've thought of the long-term future of the Court, I've not even been certain that law clerks would be part of it. In April of 1973 the Washington *Star* reported that the Justices had asked Congress for funds to replace three of the law clerks in the near future with older lawyers. Under the proposal three Justices would be allowed to hire an experienced lawyer to fill one of their present law clerk positions. "The idea," one Justice stated in Senate testimony, "would be that this person would be a considerably older, more mature, more experienced lawyer who would stay, if not a lifetime, at least for several years." The budget document further reported that the Justices "must spend time training new clerks for a half-year after their arrival in the summer," time that is ill afforded under the present case load.[46]

The proposal represented no more than a slight and limited modification of the present law clerk plan, and no Justice presently planned to displace more than one of his three clerks. Yet it unmistakably raised the question of what kind of staff and advisory help the Justices most needed. Were law clerks ultimately to give way to staffs of permanent attorneys, the Supreme Court would be a much altered institution. For in recent history the Justices had not been assisted by staffs of older lawyers, but by young men in their midtwenties, freshly cropped from the nation's law schools. Perhaps nowhere else in American government had the role of youth been so institutionalized or its responsible participation so effectively assured.

The ultimate question should always be whether and how Supreme Court law clerks have benefited the Court itself. The contribution of generations of law clerks to the Court will never be quantifiable, but it has, in my judgment, been positive (recognizing that some small dose of self-interest may prompt such an assessment). Through the years clerks have acted almost as annual messengers and liaisons to the Court from their law schools, bringing with them the latest thinking and criticism of those who most closely follow the Court's business. Many return to teach and to write, to provide their students and the public with an understanding of the Supreme Court that only an inside acquaintance can give. One of the greatest threats to the Court would be its isolation, a disease to which it is more inherently prone than the politically pressured legislature and executive. The constant ingress and egress of clerks helps prevent this isolation to a degree that a more permanent staff never could.

The very fact of a rapid staff turnover on the Court has worked to keep the reins of decision in the Justice's personal hands. Though the yearly turnover and training of new clerks does impose burdens on a Justice, its mechanics are substantially aided by one of the previous year's clerks, who stays over for a month to break new clerks into the job. And though their tenure is short, clerks represent for the Court a dependable source of top legal talent. It is not at all certain that the best older attorneys would interrupt a high-priced practice or the course of a rising career for a staff job at the Court. What is gained in experience with an older attorney might perhaps be lost in quality. Even the law clerk's chief liability—lack of experience—is often made less acute because of a prior clerkship on a lower federal court and is overcome simply because the importance and excitement of being at the Supreme Court brings with it an eagerness to impress and to learn.

One year, as opposed to a more permanent tenure, is not enough time to grow stale, and the assistance a law clerk gives to a Justice is generally zestful and high-geared. But after several years the preparation of petitions for certiorari, for example, might become a numbing and careless exercise for even the most dutiful lawyer. The research and certiorari work that clerks often perform for Justices is necessary, but it can be concentrated, lonely, and personally taxing, something that might be better done by the renewed explosions of short-term energy than by a permanently hired staff.

The most important part of my belief in the value of clerking traces to my personal experiences. At times during my clerkship, quite unsuspectingly, I fell into conversation with Justice Powell on some matter of interest, maybe the Vietnam War, or the place of the universities, the businessman, or the press in America, or the racial problems that beset our country and how they might best be resolved. Perhaps it was just a moment's discussion of some day's news headline, perhaps it had been generated by some aspect of a case. Whatever the catalyst, these conversations occasionally assumed a more general and philosophical tack, concerning themselves with where America stood in the ongoing process of civilization or what our future might hold in store or what paramount values we as a people ought to strive to possess. What the Justice said in these discussions profoundly impressed me, representing as it did the product of reflection on his work and struggles in the Depression, his service abroad in World War II, the satisfactions and frustrations during years of public service to his community and state and at the head of the organized bar. Many of my impressions sprang from a quite different source—the 1960s—the swill of the civil rights movement in the early years, followed by disillusionment, and the anguish and rejections on the campuses over Vietnam. Much of what he said I still remember and take to heart, but I remember also that he listened, not just in a polite manner, but from a profound concern. Once he told me that his clerks represented to him the future, with the new and bright and hopeful in its eye, even as unnoticeably he tempered us toward his way. I left him that year, believing that the Justice and his clerks represented a welcome fusion, the clasp of experience and expectation, something about the Court that could not be duplicated and should not be lost.

3

THE JUSTICE

It is now 8:30 A.M., and Sally Smith's car pulls up promptly. We spy in the distance a tall, trim figure in a dark suit, carrying a briefcase, walking a confident, punctual gait toward the car. Thirty seconds later the car door opens, the briefcase is handed me, Justice Powell slides in, breaks into a very quick, relaxed grin: "Good morning, chillier than I thought," or, if it is warm, "Sally, why don't we all go down to the beach today?" followed by a round of knowing laughs.

The ride to the Supreme Court will last ten minutes, through the high-rise and public housing culture of southwest Washington, then a brief stretch of gas-shortaged stations, next the prim townhouses of Capitol Hill, and last the Supreme Court, in the Capitol area itself, ruled by the traffic whistle and the construction roar. But the ride is a time of cheer, of nonbusiness, often an occasion for ribbing. "Sally, where are you hiding those gloves we gave you for Christmas?" he might ask, or "Jay, you look like you've been awake now for all of five minutes." Conversation might range from moon landings to shopping in the southwest Safeway, but the Supreme Court greets us all too soon, and a day's earnest business begins.

Justice Lewis F. Powell, Jr. had perhaps as extensive and high-placed experience in the American legal profession as any man ever appointed to the Supreme Court. Since 1937 he had been a partner in the illustrious Virginia law firm of Hunton, Williams, Gay, Powell and Gibson. In 1964–65 he had been president of the American Bar Association, and in 1969–70 president of the American College of Trial Lawyers. He had served as a member of important national commissions, some of which, such as President Johnson's Crime Commission, involved an inevitable acquaintance with the Supreme Court and its work. He had circulated, both socially and professionally, with Justices, judges of all levels, lawyers, former law clerks, and government officials who had studied, worked, or practiced before the Supreme Court and knew its business well. Yet such relationships, important as they were, never really prepared him for his new position. It took a while, he once chuckled, just to learn the Court's etiquette. "I was told, I think on about the second day, when somebody caught me in one of the corridors with my coat off . . . that Justices don't walk the corridors in their shirt sleeves."[1]

"There is another custom," he recalled in an address to the Virginia Bar Association the summer after his appointment to the Court,

that we [Mrs. Powell and I] violated the first time I handed down an opinion. The wife of a justice delivering an opinion is expected to be present in the courtroom and to be seated in a particular place. I got the word and I advised Jo and she showed up about 15 minutes late, which is not unusual in the Powell family. She immediately received a note from Justice Potter Stewart, sent there by one of the pages, saying "You just missed your husband's greatest opinion."[2]

Not surprisingly, the mail of the new Supreme Court Justice proved different from that of the corporate lawyer. He told of receiving in his chambers a package of obscene pictures, to which the sender professed great objection. In a postscript, however, the man had apologized to him for the poor quality of the reproductions, because the originals (which he had wanted to retain for his own collection) were in color.[3] The mail brought moral reprobation of his opinions as well. There arrived one day, he said,

a letter from a man in Illinois, who said his name was Lewis Powell and said he had a great, great grandfather who also had been named Lewis Powell and who had been a drummer in Lee's Army of Northern Virginia during the War Between the States. He said he had assumed that he was some kin to me until he read an opinion that I wrote in a case called *Weber* v. *Aetna* in which the Court ruled in favor of illegitimate children in certain circumstances. This gentleman said, "Now I doubt that we are kin. I never knew a Powell who was interested in illegitimate children."[4]

Beneath the novelty and busyness of arrival was the knowledge that the new position had not been accepted without reservation. When previous vacancies on the Court had occurred, he had resisted the efforts to have him considered for nomination, because, in his sixties, he was not eager to begin a new career. But genuine retirement may be an illusory goal for men of distinction, an unfortunate thought, since I often felt the Justice had tucked away some dream of a personally serene and anonymous time to spend with his family, to retravel some favorite region, and to savor the camaraderie of old and close friends. Whether that dream would have proved a restless reality is beside the point. The demands for his talents kept the vision largely unrealizable and brought an occasional wistfulness that a more personal and leisurely life had been indefinitely postponed. The compensation was to be one of but a hundred men ever to sit on the world's most powerful court. Yet even so prized a position he took with some reluctance and regret:

> The one question asked of me more than any other in the past six months by old and new friends, acquaintances and just pure strangers is whether I enjoy being on the Supreme Court of the United States. The answer is "no." I do not enjoy being away from Richmond, my friends of a lifetime, or from my home.
>
> At this point in my life I do not enjoy learning what in many respects is a new profession. I certainly do not enjoy working six and a half days a week and almost every night at a time when I had planned to be tapering off. . . .

But before there is the slightest feeling of sympathy, I will reframe the question: If one asked
not whether I enjoy my new status but whether I
would make the same decision to go on the Court
that I made last fall when this lightning struck me,
the answer most clearly would be "Yes."[5]

The word "enjoy" struck him as disconsonant with
a job whose responsibilities were so immense. A Supreme Court judgeship is perhaps the closest our
country has come to clothing mortals with deistic powers. The President and the Congress are periodically
and democratically accountable; a Justice holds his
place for life. The grand, abstract decisions of policy
made by a President and by Congress do, of course,
affect the lives and fortunes of millions, but judging
somehow seems more dramatically intertwined with
personal fate: the parties and their history lie before
the Court, and the Court pronounces who shall prevail. There is something about the words of Supreme
Court decisions that seems so philosophically solemn,
so simultaneously spirited and frustrated in their
search for an ultimate wisdom and logic, something
from which Justice Powell could and did derive enormous satisfaction and stimulation, but not what a man
of his precise way with words would ever term "enjoy-
ment."

Occasionally, the responsibility of ultimate decision
on the Supreme Court appeared so crushing, I was
relieved to be a mere law clerk. There were at least two
questions—those on the constitutionality of state anti-
abortion statutes and of capital punishment—where
the Supreme Court held life and death in the palm of

a hand, its decision to affect not merely a turn in fortune, but an ultimate fate. The abortion cases, for example, involved not only the difficult question of constitutional justifications for sweeping judicial action. It posed for the Court a conflict of the most profound moral values—the right of a woman to the control of her inner being against the right of a half-formed fetus to life. Justice Powell joined a seven-man Court majority in sharply restricting the states' authority to regulate abortions, especially those in the early stages of pregnancy.[6] Disenchantment would have followed any decision, not all of it reckless or vituperative in manner, but very much from the heart:

Dear Justice Powell,

My name is _____ and I am 15 years old—a sophomore in high school. In church the other day, we had a visiting priest who talked about abortions.

I think it is wrong for a woman to have an abortion. Some people think it's not murder for someone to have an abortion but I think it is. And when they make it murdering helpless unborn children legal, how long will it be before it is legal to kill sick old people, the mentally retarded, etc.?

The Supreme Court, it seems to me, should be protecting the rights and lives of all people, not legalize the murder of the innocent people.

Please try to do whatever you can to help. Thank you for reading my letter.

Sincerely,

_____

Whenever a man is nominated for such weighty responsibility, questions arise as to his so-called "judicial temperament," supposedly a penultimate quality for a prospective Justice, but something impossible to satisfactorily define. Most lawyers profess a feel for what "judicial temperament" is and who possesses it and who does not. But it defies precise analysis, perhaps because there is no one perfect temperament, but rather a variety of traits that may make a competent judge.

Judging is, above all, the art of decision, and decision in turn is a dual act of courage—both to make an honest judgment in the first place and to accept it, once made. The latter is especially important. Few things would be more debilitating than for a judge to relive his decisions and engage in endless self-doubt on opinions long since delivered. Justice Powell, by nature, struck an appropriate balance on this score. The conscientiousness of his effort in deciding a case seemed to assist a quieter conscience once the case came down.

In one case, *Keyes* v. *Denver School District,*[7] the Justice took, in a separate and solitary opinion, what was certain to be a controversial position. The immediate question in the case concerned the extent of the constitutional obligation of Denver, Colorado, to desegregate its public schools. In a broader sense, *Keyes* was to indicate, in the words of one commentator, "whether the Court intends to launch a major attack on school segregation in the North."[8] In his opinion Justice Powell rejected the traditional approach taken by the Court that the South had presumptively practiced one form of desegregation known as de jure, while that of the North and West was of a different character, commonly termed de facto. He urged the replacement of this distinction with "constitutional principles of national rather than merely regional application."[9] The second portion of his opinion set forth mandatory desegregation steps for recalcitrant school boards but disapproved, in the most unambiguous language by a Justice to date, the use of extended transportation of school children as a constitutionally compelled means of desegregating public schools. "Communities," he had concluded, "deserve the freedom and the incentive to turn their attention and energies to [the] . . . goal of quality education, free from protracted and debilitating battles over court-ordered student transportation."[10]

Probably no opinion caused him more self-questioning and soul-searching. As a matter of personal commitment and as a Southerner, he felt a deep urge to be generous and fair-minded on the issue of race. He was also much concerned by the effects the bitter debate on pupil transportation seemed to be having on public education. He rewrote and revised the opinion on at least ten occasions in a search for the most temperate and thoughtful approach to the problem. On the morning of June 21, 1973, *Keyes* came down. Several hours later, I entered his office to mention, perhaps presumptuously, that I knew that it was not an easy thing to have written that opinion. He looked up slowly, seemed a bit weary but relieved. "Sometimes, Jay, there are things one has to do. I suppose that, to be worthy to sit on this Court, you have to be willing to go it alone."

What I admired was his calm, a quality of quiet and

reflection that underlay his judgment, a philosophic turn of mind that almost never lapsed into resignation or indifference. Shortly after his nomination, his friends undertook to explain what would make him a great Justice. A *Richmond News Leader* editorial may have put it best: "How does one describe him? One searches for the proper adjectives. Reflective, yes. Scholarly, yes. Judicious, certainly. Incisive. Quiet. Kind. A man about whom, in Emerson's phrase, there is 'a certain toleration, a letting be and a letting do, a consideration and allowance for the faults of others, but a severity to his own.' "[11] One feature was missed —his sense of humor, especially toward himself. He salvaged many a moment with humor, without which the business of Court might have seemed unlevened and grave. He even brought his law clerk out of spells.

One day I recall being particularly frustrated, and as we rode home together, I sat silent, deep within myself, still banging against the day's problems. Suddenly, I noticed he was talking and asking what jobs I'd held before turning to law. He recalled a college summer of his own, when he had gone to work for the Department of Public Works in Richmond, which tried to use him in an engineering capacity, since he had had such a course at college. "I didn't know what in the world to do," he laughed. "My supervisors were confounded. They kept putting me on simpler and simpler jobs, and I was still helpless. Finally, they had the bright idea to stick me on ditches, where they thought it impossible to foul up. But you know, Jay, there are ditches in Richmond where the water still flows the wrong way."

This poking fun at himself extended to public occasions. In one speech, he recalled the tribulations of confirmation:

> I was cornered in the corridors of the Senate Office Building by half a dozen or more Women's Lib people who ambushed me as I came out of a Senator's office late one afternoon and I had a rough experience. I started off on the wrong foot and was completely defeated. I tried to be agreeable and I said, "Ladies, I've been married 35 years, I have three daughters and two granddaughters, and I've got to be for you." And a spokesman for the group looked at me without the slightest twinkle of humor and said, "That's what all you men say!"[12]

A good laugh may be the best and sometimes the only escape from a hard day. He reached the Court each morning between 8:30 and 9:00 A.M. and generally left between 6:30 and 7:00 P.M. He left at no set hour, only when his work reached a convenient break. As his first spring at the Court wore on, he began to depart at gradually later times, staying longer with the light, until by May he was leaving well past 7:00. I told him one evening riding home that among the many things he had successfully taught me was that no honest day's work ever ended before sundown. Some undertakings at the Court absorbed him so completely that he seemed momentarily oblivious of time and occasion. Riding to work one morning, he expressed sudden surprise at the absence of traffic. "You're forgetting George Washington's birthday," Sally kidded.

His work week routinely extended to evenings and

to weekends. He always worked six full days a week, more often seven. During the Court's term, he came to his chambers three Sundays out of four. Monday mornings often found a memorandum on my desk, evidencing thorough weekend attention to a case. Four, sometimes five, evenings a week were also devoted to the job. He would return home, and after dinner and a catchup on the evening news, spend two or three hours at work before retiring. He generally reserved for the day his sustained efforts on difficult opinions and used his evenings mainly for reading, either certiorari petitions, briefs, or opinions circulated from other Justices. I remember him walking to and from the Court, briefcase always in hand. Once he left without it, and I asked if he had forgotten anything. "No," he smiled. "But I look strangely dismembered, don't I?"

The work load of the Supreme Court has been the subject of much recent controversy that has seen the Justices themselves in divergent positions. Justice Douglas contended in one opinion that "the case for our 'overwork' is a myth" and that the Justices enjoy what amounts to a "vast leisure."[13] Some Justices have stated that whatever work-load problem the Court may have does not justify a radical alteration of its traditional jurisdiction.[14] Others, however, have seen the heavy work load as menacing to the essential quality of the Court's performance. Justice Powell's concern over the work load was not a personal matter. He had expected to assume heavy burdens as a Justice and had noted on several occasions that "I have worked six to six and a half days per week throughout my professional career."[15] He personally thrived on work and

79

found in it immense satisfaction and challenge. The
question for him was thus not the amount of time to
be devoted to the job but whether, in the time that was
humanly possible to give, a fair consideration of the
cases could be achieved. Thoughtful adjudication was
for him a necessity, not solely because of the inherent
demands of justice, but because the Supreme Court
was an institution whose authority was not democratically based but depended on Justices' powers of articulation, logic, and understanding. Hasty and careless decision forced by a crowded docket would push
the Court from reasoned judgment to rule by fiat,
undermining both the integrity of its internal consideration and the respect with which its judgments were
received. His warning was blunt:

> I would say that the Court has reached—if not
> already passed—its capacity to deal with a case-
> load which shows no prospect of leveling off.
> Even at present levels, I believe most members of
> the Court will agree that we are not always able
> to function with the care, the deliberation, the
> consultation or even the basic study which are so
> requisite to the quality and soundness of Su-
> preme Court decisions. In my view, we cannot
> continue as we are without a gradually percepti-
> ble dilution of this quality. This would be a
> tragedy for the cause of justice and indeed for our
> country.[16]

The Justice admitted freely in that speech, delivered
shortly after his first term on the Supreme Court, that
some of his impressions on the Court's work load

might be attributable to his status as a newcomer, although he did not expect a gain in experience to reverse his basic view. Still, his personal challenge that first term was a staggering one. In becoming a Supreme Court Justice, he was required almost to learn a new profession at the age of sixty-four.

At Hunton, Williams, he had been basically a corporate lawyer, specializing in matters of securities law and corporate mergers, acquisitions, and reorganizations. He had served on the boards of directors of many national corporations, Squibb, Philip Morris, and Ethyl Corporation among them. More than most corporate lawyers, he had also been something of a generalist in the field of law and public policy, serving as chairman of the Richmond Public School Board and later the State Board of Education. He was on numerous national commissions, including the Blue Ribbon Defense Panel appointed by President Nixon to study the Department of Defense and the National Advisory Committee on Legal Services to the Poor. But the shift from Hunton, Williams to the Supreme Court was still primarily one from corporate to constitutional law.[17] And, contrary to some views, constitutional law was not simply a broad and unformed policy field to be roamed and understood at will.

The impression often exists that once a man becomes a lawyer, he can knowledgeably cover the whole terrain of his profession. The law, however, encompasses a host of specialties, some of which are so removed from others as to almost constitute a separate calling. Success in different fields of law may require common patterns of legal thought and analysis, but each also carries a separate body of technical knowledge that it may take months, even years, to master. Constitutional law is no exception. Most major clauses of the United States Constitution present an impressive body of complex and often contradictory precedent as well as an initially baffling set of concepts that must be mastered before fruitful judicial inquiry can even begin. Judicial interpretation of the free speech portion of the First Amendment, for example, has produced such artful terms as "prior restraint," "chilling effect," "balancing test," "clear and present danger," and "least drastic means," to name a few, and for the equal protection clause such opaque terminology as "suspect classification," "compelling state interest," "strict scrutiny," "rational basis scrutiny," and "means scrutiny," among many others. Gaining a working grasp of such concepts and the precedents surrounding them is bound to take time.

Time, however, was something the Justice was not to have. The 1971 term was an almost unprecedentedly busy one for the Supreme Court. Far more signed Court opinions came down than in any recent term. Many of the cases were so-called "blockbusters": the questions of the constitutionality of capital punishment, of warrantless national security wiretaps, of a newsman's right to refuse to reveal confidential sources before a grand jury, were but a few of the unusually complex and publicly significant cases before the Court that term. Justice Powell, moreover, had joined a Court deeply divided on most of the critical constitutional problems before it. Many of these cases were decided by the same narrow five- or six-man majorities, of which he quite often formed a part. The inevitable result of such a large number of important and closely decided constitutional questions was that the two new Justices—Powell and Rehnquist—had to commit themselves to controversial positions and write significant Court opinions quite early in their careers. Justice Powell authored, among others, opinions denying the executive branch the right to conduct warrantless domestic security wiretaps,[18] delineating the elements of the constitutional right to a speedy trial,[19] establishing use rather than transactional immunity as satisfying the privilege against self-incrimination in cases of compelled testimony,[20] restricting rather substantially the First Amendment protections afforded pamphleteers in shopping centers,[21] and upholding, with certain preconditions, the right of Students for a Democratic Society to recognition on college campuses.[22] Each of these opinions was a major undertaking in its own right. Collectively, they constituted the substantial contribution of a freshman Justice not only to the work of the 1971 term, but to the ongoing jurisprudence of the Court.

Even before the term ended, evaluation of his work had begun. Yale Professor Alexander Bickel observed in the *New Republic* that his opinions in the immunity and unanimous-jury verdict cases were "deliberate, thoroughly professional. They reflect what in the early days of the Republic used to be called a candid mind."[23] Ironically, these same opinions provoked a quite opposite reaction from Lyle Denniston of the *Washington Evening Star,* who complained that "Lewis Powell had . . . placed himself quite immovably in the Court's right wing, and was doing so without adding either freshness or originality to that rather somber sector."[24] Fred Graham, then of *The New York Times,* in assessing the Court's new directions, thought that "Justice Powell's quick emergence as a persuasive and independent conservative was one of the significant developments of the recent term."[25] In the most probing survey of the Justice's first-term performance, constitutional scholar Gerald Gunther summed up his contribution and promise on the emerging Court:

> Court watchers—especially in the media—have linked overdramatized descriptions of shifts in substantive doctrine with exaggerated portrayals of the monolithic "single-mindedness of the Nixon team." The promise of independence and thoughtfulness in Justice Powell's work casts doubt on these perceptions and suggests that more discriminating evaluations are necessary. His performance is especially heartening, moreover, in view of the plausible assertions that eminence is beyond the reach of the newcomers to the Court.[26]

In the face of compliments the Justice was restrained, inwardly pleased but outwardly calm. He recognized that great legal stature does not come to a Justice in a day or over a term, but more likely after a decade or more of high-level performance. If his early efforts had been appreciated, that only set expectations he would try hard to maintain. One day, shortly after term's end, I rushed into his office with some kind words for him from a scholar he greatly respected. "This is terrific!" I said.

"You realize what it means," he replied.

My heart sank. "I know. That we have to work even harder."

"Oh no," he laughed. "I was just going to come in and tell you to take tomorrow off."

"Thanks," I said. "Tomorrow" was the Fourth of July.

The accomplishment of the term did not take place without some personal price. When the term ended, late in June 1972, he left wearied and drained, more so than I have ever seen him. The rest of the summer he planned to spend in Richmond, where he was given an office at the Fourth Circuit Court of Appeals in which to work. Sally and I accompanied him back for the summer, plenty tired and happy to return to our hometown for a more relaxed pace. I remember stepping into the law clerk's office at the Fourth Circuit that was to be my summer quarters. In a corner was an old hat horn of the sort my barbershop used to have just inside the door. I never wore hats, but looked at it wistfully; the horn reminded me of long August afternoons in the slow hum of that barbershop where talk was aimless and unending and worldly requirements seemed almost to wither in the heat outside.

Richmond appeared to relax Justice Powell also as he revisited old friends and returned to a home whose back porch overlooked and backyard sloped toward the rapids of the James River. There was the ease of familiar surroundings; the Justice was an obvious hometown favorite and could scarcely walk a block in downtown Richmond without meeting some expression of appreciation and support. He traveled also that summer to the American Bar Association convention in San Francisco and to the ranch of his daughter and son-in-law in Hunt, Texas. He found time to attend to personal affairs and even to sit for a portrait commissioned by his former law firm. Daily I watched 'the portrait take form: the long fingers, clear eyes, sensitive, distinct, somewhat angular features. Occasionally, when the Justice had to return to work, I was used as a surrogate, to allow the artist to capture the folds and flows of the Justice's robe, which only engulfed and overwhelmed me. The Justice enjoyed the artist's company. "You have a more difficult job than I," he told him, "because you have a subject impossible to paint." But the artist succeeded—to the satisfaction of the Justice, Mrs. Powell, and Sally alike—and the final face emerged, underneath its austerity and dignity, the everlasting potential of his smile.

The summer recess of the Supreme Court appeared to me a practical necessity. Technically, it lasts from the term's end in late June to the opening of the next term the first week in October, although by mid-September most of the Justices return to the Court and begin gearing up for the business ahead. The term of Court throws the nine Justices together day after day in an intense intellectual exchange and combat; some relief, such as a summer recess, seems necessary if human abrasions are not to develop and take their toll. Each Justice's job demands nine months of unrelenting mental effort, after which his batteries may need to be recharged. Finally, the responsibilities of decision would ideally seem to require a period of reflection, away from the insistent pressures and deadlines of the term.

Even so, the summer recess hardly qualifies as a

vacation. The ubiquitous certiorari petitions continue unabated, as do stay applications and requests for bail. For Justice Powell, the summer was also a time to study background scholarship on constitutional problems, to research and prepare important cases scheduled for the upcoming term, and to give an occasional speech. The pressures of daily decision had retreated, but he found plenty to be done. During July and August being a Justice became, he said, "more like a normal job."

But summer ended, and the Justice, much refreshed, settled into Washington by mid-September. The 1972 term began, as usual, with an almost week-long conference at which the Justices disposed of the summer's certiorari petitions. But the real effort commenced when the first opinion assignments for the cases argued in October were circulated through the Court.

The method of assigning opinions is itself important in understanding the Supreme Court. If the Chief Justice is in the majority at the conference, he assigns the opinion; if he is not, the assignment falls to the senior Associate on the majority side. The minority usually agrees informally who shall draft the dissent, though each Justice is always free to write his own concurring or dissenting views. As a general matter, the Chief Justice of the Supreme Court is *primus inter pares;* his vote weighs no more heavily than that of an Associate Justice, and his influence depends on persuasive force and mediative power among his brethren, not on titular prerogative. The assignment power, however, is something of an exception; since Justices write opinions very differently, an opinion assignment will inevitably influence the flavor of the final result and perhaps even the final vote.

The very stability of the Supreme Court rests, in fact, on a mutual trust in the matter of assignments. The Chief Justice has the great obligation to use the assignment power evenhandedly; to distribute the opinion load fairly among the Justices and not to favor one Justice with significant and conceptually exciting cases while giving another only the more tedious and obscure. The Associate Justices in turn have felt the commitment to accept and abide by the Chief's assignments. Disputes on this basic score would quickly stall the Court's progress and poison its atmosphere.

The opinion itself plays an even more crucial part both in the Court's internal operations and in the face the Court presents to the world outside. The obligation of an opinion in each case lessens considerably the dangers of arbitrary and precipitous judicial action. The Supreme Court cannot simply rule by vote and order; it must explain and persuade, in terms exposed to all, why its view is the correct one. A Justice ponders his vote more thoroughly when faced with the likelihood that he may soon be asked to justify it in an opinion in the most precise and logical way. The reasoning of his opinion will not only be scrutinized by members of the general and legal public but picked apart and lambasted by dissenting colleagues. The legacy of dissent in the Court is an honorable one: no personal bonds between Justices stand in the way of open and vigorous intellectual disagreement. This integrity of the dissenter must at all costs be maintained, for the Court, as the branch of government least democratically accountable, must remain the most intellectually so.

However indispensable opinions are to the proper function of the Supreme Court, they intrigued me more for the illumination they cast on their authors. Unlike our elected representatives, Justices do not often appear individually before the public eye, nor can they hold forth freely on public events. Notions of judicial propriety and the nature of the judicial process often prevent any public personality from developing. We thus come to know a Justice primarily from his opinions: they create his reputation; they are the phrases and thoughts he leaves to history, the part of himself that endures once he is gone. They are not lightly penned; Justice Charles Whittaker once told friends that when he wrote an opinion, he felt as if he were carving his words into granite.[27] The best opinions convey the man as well as his thought: the simplicity, eloquence, even feistiness of a Justice Black; the refinement and elegance of mind of a Harlan; the crisp, epigrammatic retorts of a Holmes. Opinion names roll familiarly off the tongue; one might mention for example, Justice Brennan's great Court opinions, *Fay* v. *Noia, Katzenbach* v. *Morgan, Baker* v. *Carr, Green* v. *County School Board, Roth* v. *United States, New York Times* v. *Sullivan,* almost as if listing a novelist's major works.

The Justices have used their clerks variously in opinion preparation. Philip Elman, a Frankfurter clerk from 1941 to 1943, observed that in opinion work,

> Frankfurter treated his clerk like a junior partner. He encouraged me to disagree with him, to

fight with him, to stick up for my ideas. We fought
over every sentence.

Sometimes paragraphs of mine emerged intact, but not very often, and when they did, they
were his, too, because we'd gone over them so
closely.[28]

Daniel J. Meador, a clerk for Justice Black in the
1954 term, presented a somewhat similar picture:

When "the Judge," as his clerks call him, is
assigned a case for an opinion he dives into reading the record and all briefs. He absolutely mas-
ters the facts and the arguments. Then he moves
into the relevant literature—cases, statutes, trea-
tises and law reviews. The clerks often read along
with him or dig out additional material and feed
it to him. The issues will be discussed intermit-
tently. After a while Black will feel that he is ready
to do a first draft of the opinion, assuming he has
not changed his mind and decided to vote the
other way, and this occasionally happens. The
draft is then turned over to the clerks, and, with
all the confidence of youth, they work it over.
Then the fun begins. The two clerks and Black
gather around his large desk and start through
the draft, word by word, line by line. This may go
on for hours. When the Judge has an opinion in
the mill, he does not drop it for anything else.
The discussion, often turning into lively debate,
will sometimes be transferred to the study in his
18th century house in Alexandria and last until
midnight. Often revisions result; sometimes a

clerk can get a word or comma accepted, but the substance and decision are never anything but Black's alone.[29]

Justice Powell used his clerks in a comparable fashion—for research and to work over drafts in head-to-head edits and analyses. The opinions were his in every way, but he made his clerks feel that they were a part of the action, sought our disagreement on his ideas for a draft, and after it was all done, readily relayed any compliments on an opinion to the clerk who had assisted him. In conversations with his clerks he referred to opinions as "our opinions," a gracious and welcome gesture, but one that belied his shaping role.

Assisting him on opinions was an exhilarating task, the chance for personal association with a superb lawyer in an important and durable enterprise. He created the experience for me, its incentives, its frustrations, and its larger and ultimate satisfactions. He never once rode or harassed a law clerk to get something done, but kept us moving at a perfect canter, and had an uncanny way of knowing whether our research and memoranda represented the very best we could do. One tried hard never to disappoint him, not because he would ever express disappointment, but because one so clearly could have read it on his face. He was a man one wanted to please, precisely because displeasure never would show in anger or pique and because his appreciation was also quiet, but marvelously generous and genuine.

His clerks also worked hard to please him, because he worked so hard to please himself. As an opinion writer, he was a mild-mannered perfectionist, quietly relentless in the pursuit of quality. He was tough-minded toward his own efforts and confronted a problem until he exhausted it and wore it down.

It was an education to watch him work on opinions. His approach stressed fundamentals, the idea that great writing came from clear language and sound structure. He distrusted words as ambiguous items that angled in on thoughts but seldom nailed them square. He wanted, above all, lucid expression and simple sentences and sacrificed many a flashier phrase to achieve them. He was fond of understatement and thought the English language debased when worked so often at a shrill and fevered pitch. Most cases before the Supreme Court had, he felt, their share of strong arguments on both sides; he insisted that his opinions openly confront opposing arguments, not as a sign of weakness, but as an obligation of candor.

Finally, he liked the connotations of the word "scholar": when he termed someone that, he had paid an honest compliment. He once told me he had been offered a professorship in law at the University of Virginia, which he had in the end declined, though not without regrets. But he sought what he termed "scholarly attributes" in opinion writing, a meticulous care in understanding and stating the facts of a case, painstaking research into its background, honest and in-context citation of precedent and authority, and a search for a principled solution to problems, together with an abjurence of the polemical and propagandistic.

It was not unusual for him to rewrite an opinion five or six times before being satisfied. Some required an even greater effort. One opinion seemed unusually unconquerable; it dragged on through the year; he rewrote it substantially at least ten times, only to announce after each rewrite that though progress had been made, the opinion needed to be redone. "Something keeps nagging me about this case," he said. "We're at the end of our tether, but it's not right. Let's keep thinking," he declared, though my mind had been rubbed raw. Finally, one April evening, I had an idea, something fundamental as to structure that might need to be altered, and I quickly telephoned him lest the idea escape. Miraculously, that evening he had hit upon the exact same solution and had pushed it several steps further. With his explanation the opinion suddenly clicked and fell into place. "I feel lots better," I stated. "Yes," he said. "I think we've won."

Among the ideas most in vogue about the Supreme Court is that Justices, as upholders of the Constitution, simply consult their own preferences and do whatever they want, free of any obligation to apply and follow principles of law. Life-tenured judges, so the theory goes, interpreting such a nebulously worded document as the Constitution and its Bill of Rights, freely follow their own instincts and issue judgments that are, in reality, more political than legal. For the First Amendment, for example, does not tell the Supreme Court how to deal with obscenity, the Fourth does not say which searches and seizures are unreasonable, the Fifth does not lay down *Miranda* warnings, nor the Fourteenth explain how to treat public discrimination against indigents and illegitimate children. The best the Court can work with is the rather vague spirit of constitutional provisions, a spirit, say many, that enthrones nothing more than a Justice's personal point of view.

This is a stubborn impression, perhaps because it is partly true. Some years ago Paul Freund rather disarmingly began a book on the Supreme Court with a story of "Old Jeremiah Smith, who began the teaching of law at Harvard after a career on the New Hampshire Supreme Court. . . . 'Do judges make law?' he [Judge Smith] repeated. 'Course they do. Made some myself.' "[30]

Justices, like the rest of us, are human; they carry their share of convictions and beliefs. And the Constitution they interpret does not ultimately establish one set of paramount values so much as it creates tension between them, between individual freedoms and our desire for efficiency and order, between governmental centralism and pluralism, between minority rights and the majority will. Supreme Court cases compel these sorts of value choices; it would be surprising indeed if, in choosing, a Justice failed to follow some code of personal belief.

There may have been times when revelations of the lawmaker's personal role would have been a shocking and disillusioning blow to the august neutrality of the nation's highest Court. Quite the opposite is true today. The Court has become heavily, perhaps unprecedently, politicized. No institution can intrude boldly and repeatedly into public controversy without fundamentally altering the public perception of it. The Supreme Court has had its say on abortion, compulsory school busing, capital punishment, obscenity, school prayers, state aid to parochial schools, police practices, and a host of issues, some so hot that the political process itself had taken shelter. However salutary and overdue the Court's reforms may have been, they were not accomplished without a price—a diminution, in the eyes of the public, of the Court as a follower of law and its ascendency as a political force. The 1968 Nixon campaign to change the course of the Court, to strengthen the "peace forces" as against "the criminal forces," and the thinly disguised "political" nature of the Haynsworth, Carswell, and subsequent confirmation battles have further bathed the Court in a political atmosphere. "It seems," a friend once told me, "as if Justices are simply super-Senators, fewer in number and longer in term."

But to say that judges make law is, as Professor Freund recognized, "not the end, but only the beginning of sophistication."[31] And to say the Court is "political" is only to confirm de Tocqueville's ancient perception that "scarcely any political question arises in the United States that is not resolved, sooner or later, into a judicial question."[32] The essential point remains, however, that the Supreme Court is *not merely* political, and those who see it as a "third political branch" voice a tempting cliché, but one that ignores everything about the Supreme Court which is truly unique. Perhaps fully as strong as a Justice's personal or political preferences are the forces that hold those preferences in check. Certainly the struggle and inquiry preceding Justice Powell's votes bespoke much more than personal impulse or preference. "This would be a much easier job," he mused, "if I could quickly vote my feelings, if I were simply free to speak my piece."

But no Justice is entirely a free agent, though the

95

forces that inhibit the expression of a Justice's personal or political beliefs may be too numerous or subtle ever to be fully understood. One of the most apparent of these forces, however, is precedent, the Court's own law, which puts flesh on the bare bones of the Constitution, and which a Justice's instincts may rebel at overruling or disingenuously distinguishing, even when he disagrees. Precedent confines a Justice's freedom of action, means that he cannot simply interpret the naked phrases of the Constitution to his will, and while it is never entirely binding, it does remind him of the principle of continuity, that disregard of the past may encourage the future's disregard of the present.

Another powerful inhibiter is simply the reality of power within the country, a knowledge that the Court cannot consistently defy public opinion or the coordinate branches of government without its own authority being undermined. There often seems to be a tacit working accommodation between the branches of government. The Court's refusal to intrude into the Vietnam War acknowledged that the declaration and conduct of war is the supreme political act, and its current jurisprudence often contains tradeoff references to economic and social regulation as generally a legislative matter, with individual civil liberties being the legitimate province of the judiciary. Defiance of public opinion may also risk changes within the Court itself, such unpopular stands as after the mid-1930s when the Justices crippled the New Deal and after the Warren era when the Court moved too quickly, in many eyes, to the defense of racial minorities and the criminally suspect.

Another less noticeable restraint on a Supreme Court Justice stems from his incentive to establish a reputation, not in the short-run sense of currying popular favor, but as a creative shaper and thinker of the law. In politics the creation of reputation is inextricably bound up with the need for survival and reelection; in the judiciary, without such pressures, reputation becomes more purely an intellectual and analytical pursuit. A reflexive dash to one form of political result, irrespective of the analytical obstacles posed, can be ruinous to a Justice's credibility and respect.

One of the foremost reputation makers and checks on the arbitrary exercise of power is, of course, a free press. A Supreme Court Justice faces not one, but a dual-level press scrutiny of his performance. There is, of course, the popular media, which performs the important job of registering public reaction to Supreme Court decisions and appraising those decisions on broader grounds of public policy. Yet there are limits to the understanding that a lay press can bring to a process so specialized and legally complex as a Supreme Court decision. For this, a professional and scholarly press measures the Court's perception of its governmental role and a Justice's intellectual candor and legal insights in producing an opinion. This press consists primarily of the law reviews at the nation's leading law schools, and its cumulative verdict is one factor in the regard in which a Justice will ultimately be held. Its leading luminaries, most often, though not exclusively, professors of constitutional law, are denominated "Court-watchers" and perform for the Court a function not unlike a veteran and sophisticated commentator such as James Reston does for the Presidency. The commentary can be sharp and unsparing, and some very fine Justices have felt its heat, as, for example, Justice Brennan did for the historical treatment of habeas corpus in *Fay* v. *Noia*,[33] Justice Stewart for his rationale in an opinion denying counsel to accused persons in preindictment lineups,[34] and Justice Powell in a *Columbia Law Review* article that found his analysis of the right to a speedy trial "less than gratifying. The result is a right debilitated, its components askew."[35]

Some scholarly commentators on the Supreme Court have hoped for "genuinely principled" decision making, "reaching judgment on analysis and reasons quite transcending the immediate result that is achieved."[36] This is not entirely a vain aspiration, for the great Justices have not always been figures of political consistency. Their work has achieved a thematic coherence rather than an ideological predictability. Justice Black's view of constitutional requirements meant, in political terms, a so-called "liberal" view of the protections afforded the exercise of free speech and a staunchly "conservative" support of police search and seizure powers. Justice Harlan was equally difficult to characterize politically: his views of our system of federalism led him to "conservative" or "liberal" positions on much the same issue, depending on whether the Court sought constitutional restrictions of state or federal power. Ultimately, greatness rests more on how the Justice applies his craft than on his ideological bent. The greatest Justices of recent history—Black, Brandeis, Frankfurter, Harlan, Holmes, Hughes, and Warren have spanned, both individually and collectively, a rather broad part of the political spectrum.

Justice Powell resisted the spillover of political labels to judicial figures; labeling, he thought, denóted a reflexive, Pavlovian way of going about things, quite the antithesis of what a Supreme Court Justice was supposed to be. "The truth is," he admonished me very early, "I do not regard myself as conservative or liberal." I soon learned to believe him. Occasionally, I found myself asked, before a case had come down, how I thought the Justice was going to vote. It would have been, had I known it, a cardinal breach of confidence ever to reveal this, but, in truth, I often could not guess with any real assurance.

A lifelong friend once told of the Justice in his prep school days, milling with friends at lunch hour, "munching sandwiches as only boys can munch them. The vast majority of us were going to the University of Virginia. And we said, 'Lewis, of course you are coming with us.' He said that he would be going to Washington and Lee. And afterwards he and I were puttering around somewhere on the grounds and I said, 'Why are you going to Washington and Lee?' He said, 'There are just too many of us going to the University of Virginia and I think I should strike out on my own.' "[37]

It was ironic that commentators on the Justice's early Supreme Court career stressed the same quality of independence. The two most prescient scholarly articles on the Justice, that of Professor A. E. D. Howard, of the University of Virginia,[38] and of Professor Gerald Gunther, of Stanford, each concluded that the

Justice would strike his own legal course. Gunther noted that "there are indications of some independence in the voting record. It was Justices White and Stewart who most commonly cast the decisive votes when the Court was closely divided. But Justice Powell departed from the other Nixon appointees in a significant handful of cases."[39] *Newsweek*, in an article on the Court, thought:

> Powell has proved himself perhaps the most unpredictable of the Nixon Justices. He voted *for* the sweeping abortion-reform decision and has also written the majority opinions in rulings that would have to be counted as setbacks for the Administration: one that bars state aid to parochial schools and, ironically, a decision that bars the President from wiretapping domestic radicals without first seeking court orders.[40]

It was his wiretap opinion that provoked the greatest surprise, because in an article in the *Richmond Times-Dispatch*, shortly before his nomination, he branded the outcry against wiretapping as "a tempest in a teapot" and the charge of civil liberties repression in America as "standard leftist propaganda. . . . There are only a few hundred wiretaps annually, and these are directed against people who prey on their fellow citizens or who seek to subvert our democratic form of government. Law-abiding citizens have nothing to fear."[41]

But the views of the private citizen and the later Supreme Court Justice do not always coincide. Judge Jerome Frank once commented pithily that "When I woke up one morning a federal court judge, I found myself about the same person who had gone to bed the night before an S.E.C. Commissioner."[42] It is not, however, that simple. No Justice completely transforms and reshapes his beliefs upon ascending to the high Court, but there is a vast difference between an opinion offered with knowledge of its negligible practical consequences and the expression of views that will shortly become the law of the land. In the case of *United States* v. *United States District Court* the government claimed that the President's powers to protect the national security justified wiretapping domestic threats to that security without prior judicial approval. Justice Powell responded in a way oddly unlike private citizen Powell in the *Richmond Times-Dispatch:*

> History abundantly documents the tendency of Government—however benevolent and benign its motives—to view with suspicion those who most fervently dispute its policies. Fourth Amendment protections become the more necessary when the targets of official surveillance may be those suspected of unorthodoxy in their political beliefs. The danger to political dissent is acute where the Government attempts to act under so vague a concept as the power to protect "domestic security." Given the difficulty of defining the domestic security interest, the danger of abuse in acting to protect that interest becomes apparent. Senator Hart addressed this dilemma in the floor debate on 2511(3): "As I read it—and this is my fear—we are saying that the President, on his motion, could declare—name your favorite poi-

son—draft dodgers, Black Muslims, the Ku Klux Klan, or civil rights activists to be a clear and present danger to the structure or existence of the Government." The price of lawful public dissent must not be a dread of subjection to an unchecked surveillance power. Nor must the fear of unauthorized official eavesdropping deter vigorous citizen dissent and discussion of Government action in private conversation. For private dissent, no less than open public discourse, is essential to our free society.[43]

What travels the mind of a man on the eve of momentous decision is sometimes impossible to unravel. With him this was particularly true, because his philosophy of life was not a simple thing. Perhaps because he began work in the Depression and gave four years of his life to World War II, he was tough-minded toward requirements for personal and national survival. Yet at the same time he possessed great personal kindness and compassion. He could be fatalistic and resigned to adverse turns of events and he understood, in Robert Burn's phrase, how "the best laid plans of mice and men gang aft agley." Yet he also held strongly to notions of individual dignity and responsibility. On occasion, he would lay down what seemed a very clear and emphatic personal credo, with all the trappings of definitiveness, but which failed in the end to explain him or the diverse positions that he took.

One such statement that in fact revealed important aspects of his thinking was his 1972 Prayer Breakfast

Speech at the annual convention of the American Bar Association in San Francisco. There he carved his basic vision of citizen discipline and responsibility:

> And as to values, I was taught—and still believe—that a sense of *honor* is necessary to personal self respect; that *duty,* recognizing an individual subordination to community welfare, is as important as rights; that *loyalty,* which is based on the trustworthiness of honorable men, is still a virtue; and that *work and self discipline* are as essential to individual happiness as they are to a viable society. Indeed, I still believe in *patriotism*—not if it is limited to parades and flag waving, but because worthy national goals and aspirations can be realized only through love of country and a desire to be a responsible citizen.[44]

From this vision stemmed his conviction that individuals, in all circumstances of life, remain accountable for their personal conduct. During the 1960s he resisted vigorously the voguish explanations contrived to divest individuals of personal responsibility for their actions. He empathized with the formidable obstacles faced by the dispossessed in our country, but he did not believe that branding America a "sick" or "materialist" or "racist" or "imperialist" society excused disobedience to the law or a refusal to undertake an honest effort at personal betterment. It was too easy, he thought, to blame personal fallibility on societal shortcomings. In 1966 he saw in the violence and civil disobedience attending civil rights protest and the incipient antiwar movement a fundamental dissolution in citizen discipline and responsibility to the social fabric:

It is true that the Negro has had, until recent years, little reason to respect the law. The entire legal process, from the police and sheriff to the citizens who serve on juries, has too often applied a double standard of justice. . . .

The Vietnam War and the role of this country in Asia are indeed subjects of grave national concern. They should be responsibly debated and questioned—as they have before the Congressional Committees, on the campus and in the media—and no one should stigmatize the dissenter's vital role in this democratic process. . . .

[But] those drawn to civil disobedience by the worthiness of causes might reflect that the doctrine is urged as one of universal application, with its moral imperatives and techniques available to all. If sit-ins and massive demonstrations are justified for the 'worthy,' they are equally justified for the 'unworthy,' as under this doctrine each man may determine which laws are unjust, and each has the 'moral duty' to disobey them. . . .

The logical and inescapable end of civil disobedience is the destruction of public order, and in the anarchy which follows, all liberty would be lost.[45]

As the Vietnam war cooled and the turbulence of the 1960s at least temporarily subsided, he perceived a different threat to his ideal of individualism in the

new ethic that sanctioned the dropping out and with-
drawal from society and where, as he put it, "one's
chief allegiance is to . . . his own desires." He deplored
the "manifestations of unanchored individualism in
the new mores of our time," and saw in some contemporary concepts of sexual permissiveness and the drug
culture "excessively tolerant views toward personal
conduct."[46] It was a tolerance that threatened his
philosophy of individual worth and duty as much as
the tolerance for the disregard of law had the decade
before.

But knowing that he held what some would call a
stern and traditionalist code of personal conduct
seemed to me only a first step in understanding him.
His prescription of individual obligation and fulfill-
ment was irrevocably locked into a broader national
outlook. Democratic institutions existed for the purpose of maximizing individual freedoms, the most
precious gift, in his view, that a state could confer on
its citizens. These institutions were meant to with-
stand vigorous buffeting and dissent; yet their everlasting survival was not assured without restraint and
sacrifice on the part of those who lived under them.
While he believed quite fervently in individual freedoms, he was not without a sense of institutional
fragility; he feared, for example, that universities
could be destroyed as havens of free inquiry by the
shrill exchange of slogan and dogma, that the great
benefits of a free and vigilant press might sour without
its simultaneous commitment to accuracy and impar-
tiality, that the capability of courts for fair and creative
problem solving could be lessened by the excessive-
ness with which litigants resort to them, and that the

capacity of our officials to lead and to govern might be crippled under insistent and vocal outpourings of distrust. The ethic of individual restraint and discipline —of honor, patriotism, duty, and diligence—that had enabled the country to live long and successfully with democratic institutions, ran deep within the American soul, he often said, within "millions of decent citizens who have these values, Jay," despite repeated assaults on them, sophisticated disenchantments, and the examples of public leaders who proved less than exemplary.

Those institutions bearing intimately on the individual's private life were no less important to him than the strength of public ones. No individual can ever subsist within himself, he emphasized, but needs an intimate personal identification and belonging with the family and community life about him. Once I asked him what satisfactions being a Supreme Court Justice and the assurance of an honest place in the nation's history had brought, and his response seemed surprisingly matter-of-fact. "Oh, I don't mean to say it's not very meaningful, Jay. Of course it is. You may be too young and star-struck to realize this now," he said, "but the personal sustenance from family and friends will be more gratifying to you than your work." He meant this, and once lamented the decline of family and community ties thus:

Today, we are being cut adrift from the type of humanizing authority which in the past shaped the character of our people.

I am thinking, not of governmental authority, but rather the more personal forms we have known in the home, church, school, and community. These personal authorities once gave direction to our lives. They were our reference points, the institutions and relationships which molded our characters.

We respected and grew to maturity with teachers, parents, neighbors, ministers, and employers —each imparting their values to us. These relationships were something larger than ourselves, but never so large as to be remote, impersonal, or indifferent. We gained from them an inner strength, a sense of belonging, as well as of responsibility to others.

This sense of belonging was portrayed nostalgically in the film "Fiddler on the Roof." Those who saw it will remember the village of Anatevka in the last faint traces of sunset on Sabbath eve. There was the picture of Tevye, the father, blessing his family, close together around their wooden dining-room table. They sang what must have been ancient Hebrew hymns, transmitted from family to family through untold generations. The feeling of individual serenity in the common bond of family life was complete.[47]

The threat to these traditional institutions is clear enough; the increasing divorce rate, the turn away from the church, and the loss of a spirit of community in the urban environment have been much discussed and analyzed. He viewed such trends with disquiet, fearful that we, as a people, might be losing our rootedness and unifying bonds. His vision hearkened to a more personal life, to the restoration of sensitivity and personalism in our community lives as much as to the harsher imperatives and dislocations of great social reform. As he said in opposition to extensive, court-compelled busing of schoolchildren for public school desegregation:

> Neighborhood school systems, neutrally administered, reflect the deeply felt desire of citizens for a sense of community in their public education. Public schools have been a traditional source of strength to our Nation, and that strength may derive in part from the identification of many schools with the personal features of the surrounding neighborhood. Community support, interest, and dedication to public schools may well run higher with a neighborhood attendance pattern: distance may encourage disinterest. Many citizens sense today a decline in the intimacy of our institutions—home, church, and school—which has caused a concomitant decline in the unity and communal spirit of our people. I pass no judgment on this viewpoint, but I do believe that this Court should be wary of compelling in the name of constitutional law what may seem to many a dissolution in the traditional, more personal fabric of their public schools.[48]

When he was confirmed for the Court, there was but one vote against him, that of Fred Harris, populist Senator from Oklahoma, who thought that a man who had moved among "the rich, the comfortable, the approved" could not understand the plight of the down-trodden individual the Constitution was meant to protect.[49] The Justice may have seemed, at first blush, the perfect patrician; he was slender and erect, refined and mannered, with the quiet and unpretentious warmth of the quintessential host. He was precise and careful in dress and in word; I never once heard him speak an ungrammatical phrase. I had to laugh one day when an employee of the Court came and asked me, "Hey, that Judge Powell of yours, has he ever blown his cool?" "I guess everybody does," I answered. "But in his own way."

There was another view of the nominee, rather unlike that of Senator Harris, given by Jean Camper Cahn, a black woman who had worked with Mr. Powell in establishing the OEO Legal Services Program. Jean Camper Cahn is an aggressive, articulate, hard-nosed black spokesman, whose natural instincts could not have drawn her to endorse a white, genteel Southerner for a seat on "that court of last resort to which I and my people so frequently must turn as the sole forum in which to petition our government for a redress of grievances." Indeed, she acknowledged that she and the nominee might disagree on many subjects. Yet, somehow, across the gulf, a rapport had flourished, one that ultimately led Ms. Cahn to give to the Senate Judiciary Committee the most eloquent and insightful portrait yet produced of the man:

> He has come to symbolize the best that the profession has to offer—a man imbued, even driven, by a sense of duty, with a passion for the law as the embodiment of man's ordered quest for dignity. Yet he is a man so curiously shy, so deeply sensitive to the hurt or embarrassment of

another, so self-effacing that it is difficult to rec-
oncile the public and private man—the honors
and the acclaim with the gentle, courteous, sensitive spirit that one senses in every conversation,
no matter how casual. . . .

My support is based upon the fact that I am
drawn inescapably to the sense that Lewis Powell
is, above all, humane; that he has a capacity to
empathize, to respond to the plight of a single
human being to a degree that transcends ideolo-
gies or fixed positions. And it is that ultimate
capacity to respond with humanity to individualized instances of injustice and hurt that is the best
and only guarantee I would take that his conscience and his very soul will wrestle with every
case until he can live in peace with a decision that
embodies a sense of decency and fair play and
common sense.[50]

During the time I worked for him his favorite topic
of conversation was simply people, high and low, good
and bad, in all the astonishing states into which life
had thrown them. There was a tolerance in his description of others. He traced the hopes and disappointments of his characters, almost as if he were one
of them and lived along with them in his stories. He
told laughingly of a salty hunting guide on the eastern
shore of Maryland giving the Supreme Court "the
dickens," and admiringly of a man who found in an
auto graveyard a spare part for two dollars that would
otherwise have cost fifty, and very sadly of a lifelong
garage attendant who found the screeching and wheel-

ing of the cars so intolerable, he finally had to quit and rest his nerves. He asked about people, if my friend had yet made it into law school, if a child of the elevator operator at the Court had recovered from the flu. He spoke of the change in fortunes of people he knew, of a shy boy who became a great philanthropist, of a college standout whose potential failed to flower. He relished human uniqueness, the whole rich tapestry of life and the characters that moved therein. He often pondered the kinds of fates and forces that placed "John" here and "Jim" there. Mostly, he treated me to a wealth of feeling observation on human nature such as I had not seen before.

Among his best opinions were those where an individual injustice seemed uppermost, and to this he responded warmly. Both the lawyer and the humanist went to work—to allow an alien the right to practice law in our country,[51] an illegitimate child to recover benefits for the death of his father,[52] a Mississippi black to tell his story in court,[53] or to allow a one-time indigent defendant the protections under Kansas garnishment law "needed to keep himself and his family afloat."[54] These opinions seemed effective, not only because they were compassionate but because they were reined in by his lawyer's instinct, his feeling disciplined by the vigor of structure and thought, as a Mozart symphony is the more moving because it is restrained. I recalled again the words of Jean Camper Cahn—"to respond with humanity to individualized instances of injustice and hurt"—and thought them realized.

Serving Justice

Like so many others at the Supreme Court, Justice
Powell had long been a fan of the Washington Redskins, an informed but unfanatic follower who knew
the names of the linebackers, but not the offensive
linemen. The Redskins traditionally repaid their fans
with a long string of losing seasons, and the Justice
was among the sufferers. He occasionally relived those
losses—in agony only a Redskin fan would know—
telling of Sonny Jurgensen and his golden arm bringing the Redskins last minute rallies, falling desperate
inches and seconds short. "Sonny is always the show-
man," he told me. "He keeps your hopes going right
up to the bitter end." The Justice had been for years
a Redskin season ticket holder, but he surrendered his
tickets on arrival at the Court, then decided to retrieve
them. When Jurgensen injured his ankle at the beginning of the 1972 season, the Justice added to the athlete's fan mail, wishing him a speedy return to action.
But even without Jurgensen the Redskins enlivened
the Justice's first fall on the Court with a successful
season and an eventual trip to the Super Bowl. Yet,
win or lose, the Justice was not without coaching
suggestions as we rode to work the next morning. I
once told him that Monday-morning quarterbacking
wasn't cricket. He smiled, remarking quizzically that
since everyone could second-guess his own decisions,
wasn't he entitled to do some of the same?

He relaxed with sports. He was a determined athlete
in his school days, once even a semipro baseball
player. A friend remembers him at McGuire's prep
school as a first baseman. "I can see him now with the
same lanky frame . . . stretching off first base, and there
was always a damn gap between the bottom of his

trousers and the top of his socks."[55] As he grew older, he turned from baseball and basketball to occasional hunting and tennis. But he spent endless hours coaching his son, watching him progress from the neighborhood team, the Rothesay Rebels, to a standout starting quarterback at his own alma mater Washington and Lee. Once he mentioned that, given his choice of careers, there was nothing he would rather have been than a professional athlete. Every contest, he said, had a quick and indelible outcome. Athletes, moreover, were the real idols of a nation craving for visible, physical heroes and frustrated over the ambiguities and complexities of national problems. Few things, he thought, were more satisfying than watching a drama of physical coordination and grace. I remember objecting, more earnestly than his tone required. "Mr. Justice, you're not injury-prone, you don't have to negotiate an annual contract, you never get booed coming off the field. And, besides, think of what a Supreme Court Justice can accomplish."

"Maybe so," he laughed. "But nobody ever retires your number."

Upon occasion, the Justice and Mrs. Powell invited the staff to their apartment for cocktails or dinner. These gatherings were great fun and offered us all the chance to put office frustrations in a more jovial perspective. Invariably, the occasions were enlivened by Mrs. Powell, a woman with a remarkable talent for decor and furnishings and the gift of putting guests immediately at ease. She was always a favorite of mine because we laughed at the same things. One evening she and the Justice invited me for dinner, and one of the items served was fresh asparagus. I made what I now know was the horrendous mistake of eating only the tips and leaving the stalks on my plate. To this day she won't let me forget it.

"You may have passed up your chance for fresh asparagus for a while," she once teased.

Though his work as a Supreme Court Justice was even harder than his previous work had been, at least, she said, he was more frequently at home. His diversions were few. Judging on the Supreme Court can be a solitary occupation, more lonely for one such as the Justice who kept an active schedule prior to coming on the bench. His had been a life of friendship and travel, seeing clients, attending directors' meetings as well as conventions and seminars of the organized bar. He worked often in concert with the country's upper echelons of lawyers and businessmen. He saw himself as activist and partisan, in behalf of clients' causes, political candidates, ABA programs, and community projects. He spoke vigorously and emphatically on national issues that included civil disobedience, the necessity for the control of crime, and a strong national defense.

Suddenly this had changed. The excitement of competition and partisanship was replaced by an obligation of detached and neutral judgment. The collegial associations of the prominent lawyer yielded inevitably to the pressure for aloofness on the judge. The hours of travel became long hours at the desk, alone in thought and in his reading. Much of judging on the Supreme Court is solitary and intense intellectual labor, one of the world's great intellectual and philosophical experiences, but one for which the Justice sacrificed much in the vigor and variety of his lifestyle. "The truth is," he once said, "that I'd rather be a lawyer than a judge. I was never in any doubt as a lawyer as to which side I was on."[56]

Though I worked for him as judge, it is impossible not to remember him as a lawyer. He had a banking friend who always used to call him "the barrister," the title that seemed to fit him best. He saw lawyering as an artisan trade, perhaps because he began it in the Depression and had once offered his services to a Richmond firm for nothing, explaining simply that "I just wanted somewhere to practice law."

He pronounced the word "lawyer" with particular care and pride. "Bill is a fine lawyer," he often said, if he admired the job a clerk had done. He had learned life's lessons from the law, lessons he related to his clerks in timely anecdotes, best called "lawyerisms." Once, in a memorandum for him, I had overlooked an important and elemental issue and sat red with embarrassment when he informed me of this. He, however, seemed unruffled and recalled the time when he had just arrived at Hunton, Williams, as a young attorney eager to make a first impression. It was nearly his first case; he had researched it exhaustively, he thought, and found a Virginia precedent, right on point, holding for his side. But disaster awaited. His brief had been sent to a New York law firm with whom Hunton, Williams had been working on the case, and the law firm had returned it promptly to his senior partner with the notation that the precedent had been completely overruled by a recent Virginia statute. He had been mortified. "There's not a lawyer in the country who hasn't occasionally missed things," he explained. "I still dream about that mistake."

Another "lawyerism" rescued me from an even more delicate situation. We had had differing views on a particular case, one about which I felt strongly. I had argued my side one afternoon, researched it further that evening, and appeared early next morning armed with books and rhetoric to which he listened and responded patiently for almost an hour. At the end he said, "I'm sorry, but I simply disagree." When I rose to leave, it suddenly dawned on me that my remarks had been unusually heated and persistent and had carried somewhat beyond the bounds of civil discussion. I felt sickened that, for the first time, he would think me disrespectful. But he spoke before I reached the door. "There's absolutely nothing to worry about," he assured me. "You wouldn't be worth much as a lawyer if you weren't contentious."

The Justice never thought of himself as holding a regional seat or being a regional representative to the Supreme Court. In fact, he mentioned once that carefully balanced sectional representation was not essential to the Court's proper functioning. What he did hope was that Justices would come to the Court from a broad range of backgrounds, from government service and political life, from prior state and federal judgeships, from the great law schools, and from the practicing bar. Amidst the praise and support for his appointment, the most he would say was, "It seems a wise thing to have some practicing lawyers appointed to the Court."

Perception of a lawyer's working habits almost invisibly conditioned his conduct as a judge. Lawyering required a "patience with detail," he might say, or, when work was heavy, "the best lawyers have never worked by the clock." The frequent comparisons between Justice Powell and the late Justice Harlan stemmed from the fact that both were "lawyer's judges," with backgrounds of thorough and precise articulation in the best traditions of the private bar. It has been observed often that legal training and professional legal attitudes and associations have a conservative impact, that they inculcate a preference for stability and a view of reform only as a properly channeled and slowly evolving process. Professor Howard saw this legal training as the formative force in Justice Powell's philosophy:

> Legalism tends to conservatism in the sense that law is a conserving force, one that looks to rules and accepted modes. No man has spent his life more squarely in this legalistic tradition than Lewis Powell, who comes to the Court, at age 64, with habits and attitudes that cannot fail but be shaped by conspicuous success and recognition at working within these accepted legal modes.[57]

The most succinct expression of the Justice's philosophy of the Court's role confirmed this:

> (1) I believe in the doctrine of separation of powers. The courts must ever be mindful not to encroach upon the areas of the responsibilities of the legislative and executive branches.
> (2) I believe in the Federal system, and that both State and Federal courts must respect and preserve it according to the Constitution.
> (3) Having studied under then Professor Frank-

furter, I believe in the importance of judicial restraint, especially at the Supreme Court level.
This means as a general rule, but certainly not in
all cases, avoiding a decision on constitutional
grounds where other grounds are available.

(4) As a lawyer I have a deep respect for precedent. I know the importance of continuity and
reasonable predictability of the law. This is not to
say that every decision is immutable, but there is
normally a strong presumption in favor of established precedent.

(5) Cases should be decided on the basis of the
law and facts before the Court. In deciding each
case, the judge must make a conscious and determined effort to put aside his own political and
economic views and his own predilections and to
the extent possible to put aside whatever subtle
influences may exist from his own background
and experience.

And, finally, although all the three branches of
Government are duty bound to protect our liberties, the Court, as the final authority, has the
greatest responsibility to uphold the law and to
protect and safeguard the liberties guaranteed all
of our people by the Bill of Rights and the 14th
Amendment.[58]

The caution and restraint of that statement were, in
the last analysis, not so much a product of the lawyer
as a part of the man himself. He taught, by example,
a serenity in the face of ambiguity and uncertainty,
something I found it difficult to achieve. "We shall
see," he would sometimes say, when I rushed to ask

if such and such would occur. His caution made him believe that careless and ebullient optimism could be a dangerous state. Occasionally, he chided me as being too hopeful an evaluator of the progress of work in his chambers and once circulated a memorandum to his staff to dispel "the euphoria of my friend Jay, who keeps telling me that we are in 'great shape.' "

His reserve may have owed something to the reigning ethos of his state and region. Virginia had, for most of his lifetime, been governed by the Byrd organization, a clique of gentlemen aristocrats who, in their finer hours, imparted a tone of civility and tolerance to life in the Old Dominion. One notable exception was that of "massive resistance," where the Byrd organization in the late 1950s chose to close public schools rather than accept racial integration. That was not the aim of the then Mr. Powell, who from 1952 to 1961 had been Chairman of the Richmond Public School Board. In the words of one prominent observer, "His primary concern was to keep the schools of Virginia open and to preserve the public education system for all pupils." That a poisonous racial climate did not envelop Richmond was "in large measure due to the calm leadership, the perceptive judgment, and the open-minded and fair attitude which exemplified Mr. Powell's school board incumbency."[59]

Another man who had played a moderating role in those years was John Stewart Battle, Governor of Virginia from 1950 to 1954. The Justice had admired the former Governor's bearing in public life and, when Battle died in 1972, accepted an invitation to write his memorial for the annual report of the Virginia Bar Association. It has often been noted that tributes are as much a measure of the author as of the man to whom he pays respect. I thought that in describing John Battle, the Justice had provided, quite unwittingly, a marvelous self-portrait as well:

> I remember John Battle as the pre-eminent gentleman. He brought trust and integrity, gentleness and tolerance, to the service of the state and nation. We will miss him—his warm humor, his courtly manner, the mellow wisdom he gave us all in hard or heated times. A nation whose public life all too often boils over with rancour and mistrust will miss its John Battles.
>
> John Battle was the symbol of moderation; he came to politics to heal and to harmonize, not to rend or to rupture. By temperament and conviction, he was a traveller of the broad middle way of American politics. His integrity and trustworthiness more than once tempered the animosities of contesting factions. . . .
>
> It was in our state's trying period of the late 1950's that Governor Battle's best instincts as a lawyer and champion of education came forward. He firmly rejected both defiance of law and the closing of public schools as a means of preventing racial integration.
>
> Though politics often abounds with self-inflating gestures, the characteristic qualities of John Battle's public service were its modesty and self effacement. His friends and admirers often pushed him for positions which he honestly did not want or seek. . . . When President Eisenhower appointed him to the Civil Rights Commission in

1957, the characteristic answer was: "I felt that in good conscience I could not decline."

Virginia and its finest men have embodied a Jeffersonian spirit, the humane vision that still springs from Monticello and the hills of Albemarle, and the consciousness there of the supremacy and dignity of the individual man. Surely John Battle reflected to a remarkable degree those qualities of humaneness and respect for the individual, which are the hallmarks of our cherished Western civilization.

His place in the history of Virginia is secure. His stature as a lawyer in the great tradition of the Virginia bar will long be remembered. Perhaps that which would please him the most will be the enduring affection of his family and friends.[60]

As my time with him drew to a close, I was undecided whether to teach or to practice law. He became during the moments of decision something of a career counselor, exploring all paths but dictating none. "What you really need to do, Jay," he said, "is to get married." He thought me sadly incapable of caring for myself. My apartment, he had heard, was in a state of disarray, and he had learned, with incredulity, that I had been cooking for myself. Jay "tried spaghetti last night with disastrous results," he once wrote a mutual friend. "It reminded him of glue."

The day came—I got engaged. We set the wedding for June 30, 1973, shortly after I thought the term of Court would end. My fiancée came to Washington each weekend, and the Justice could not resist the chance for fun. "Lossie," he would say, with his very gravest look, "I'm not at all certain the Court will adjourn in time for the wedding. If I need Jay here with me in the closing moments, I know you'll understand." Lossie looked very concerned, whereupon the Justice broke out laughing. "We'll get you married somehow," he promised. "If worst comes to worst, I'm empowered to perform the ceremony here in my chambers."

He enjoyed the wedding's approach. "Grooms are only incidental to a wedding ceremony," he warned. "Don't insert yourself in any arrangements. The ladies will always outmaneuver you because they'll devote full time." During May and June, the closing months of the term, I was kept much too busy even to think about marriage. New projects appeared faster than the old were done. Finally, the term ended, several days before the wedding, and I headed quickly home. The departure seemed rushed and fatigued, a strangely emotionless end to an experience that had meant so much. Driving home, I regretted leaving the Justice without one good, final conversation, to relive old moments and express my thanks. But there had been no complete good-bye, I thought; getting married seemed to have caught me up before the clerkship had let go.

Saturday evening of the reception: a gay, spinning, half-remembered affair. Snapshot smiles and faces, distant laughs, and spilling champagne. But my two co-clerks, Bill Kelly and Larry Hammond, were there, and Sally Smith, too, letting the good times roll. Suddenly, I caught the Justice walking over from across the room. He was grinning broadly as he shook my hand. "Well," he said, "we all made it, didn't we?" For just a moment, I tried to be serious and grateful. Don't mention it, he seemed to be saying. "Go have fun."

4

THE COURT

Just inside the main entrance to the United States Supreme Court is a bronze, sculptured replica of nine Justices behind the bench, listening intently and eternally to the words of some imaginary counsel the sculptor failed to provide. The impression is of a Supreme Court everlasting, but the faces are familiar and well remembered: Chief Justice Warren at center, flanked by Justices Black and Douglas, in turn flanked by Justices Clark and Harlan, with Justices Brennan, Stewart, White, and Goldberg at the wings. I never looked at that sculpture unambiguously. Was it a demonstration of institutional strength and durability, or was it instead a temporal portrait of the Warren Court in 1965, of judicial activism at flood tide?

How much has changed since then, I once thought. In the late 1960s, a time of rising public fear of crime, the Warren Court expanded the rights of the accused. At a time of national racial violence the Court stood fast in its protection of minority rights. By 1968 candidate Nixon was making of the Court a major campaign issue:

> The *Miranda* and *Escobedo* decisions of the High Court have had the effect of seriously hamstringing the peace forces in our society and strengthening the criminal forces. . . . From the point of view of the criminal forces, the cumulative impact of these decisions has been to set free patently guilty individuals on the basis of legal technicalities. The tragic lesson of guilty men walking free from hundreds of courtrooms across the country has not been lost on the criminal community.[1]

As often happens when the subject of the Supreme Court enters the political arena, distortion took place. The "peace forces, criminal forces" matchoff meant to many that the Warren Court was deliberately out to encourage crime. The fashionable appeal was now for "judicial self-restraint," not so much as a neutral ideal, but because the Court's most recent activist excesses happened to run in a liberal direction. Calls for "strict constructionists" went forth, ignoring the fact that a *truly* strict construction of many constitutional clauses might produce a quite liberal result. But the thrust of such slogans was clear enough, and the new President very quickly found himself in a position to implement his campaign message. After several false starts and mishaps, four "Nixon Justices" arrived on the High Bench, the Court was popularly dubbed "the Nixon

Court," and friends and foes of the old Warren Court waited expectantly for their worst fears or hopes to be confirmed.

That at least was the popular picture, one of abrupt about-face on the part of the Supreme Court. As a clerk, I would read or hear commentary on the Court and wonder whether I was not caught up in something quite sudden and catastrophic. The emphasis of the commentary was on change and more change, in a way that would seriously impair the Warren heritage. Practically every major newspaper and periodical ran articles on the Court whose titles bespoke their content: *Time Magazine:* "The Nixon Radicals"; *Newsweek:* "The Nixon Way"; *The New York Times:* "SUPREME COURT, IN RECENT TERM, BEGAN SWING TO THE RIGHT THAT WAS SOUGHT BY NIXON"; *Washington Post:* "NIXON HAS UNIQUE OPPORTUNITY IN SUPREME COURT NOMINATIONS"; *Washington Evening Star:* "AS ANTICIPATED, NIXON MAJORITY A COURT REALITY."[2] The law reviews seconded the refrain, though in more qualified fashion, and spoke of the "emerging Nixon majority" and the "Burger Court" in a way that presaged the coming of a new and quite different judicial era.[3]

There were, to be sure, some cautionary notes. Melvin Wulf, legal director of the ACLU, wrote for *Civil Liberties* "an optimistic appraisal" of the Burger Court's October 1971 term. The Justices, said Wulf, "share a common understanding that there is a line beyond which they will not tolerate tampering with fundamental constitutional principles. It's not my line, but it is probably—hopefully—a tolerable line."[4] Constitutional scholar Gerald Gunther struck a similar chord: "I would say that there is not nearly so much to the about-face assertions as some newspaper columnists and political leaders believe. The Court's work notoriously resists oversimplification."[5] But the accent of the early 1970s was mostly on change, partly because Court watching is a more exciting pastime if large doctrinal shifts can be pointed to, partly because the atmosphere of change on the Court bore such close surface resemblance to emerging political issues and alliances within the country, and partly, of course, because specific recent cases could be cited with some assurance that they would have been decided differently by the nine men of 1965.

Yet there was irony in the depictions of change. Many of those who dramatized the differences between the Warren and Burger Court also highlighted the undifferentiated character of the Justices who were bringing the change about. "The single-mindedness of the Nixon team threatens the image of the Court as an independent institution," wrote the *New Republic.* Most often the Nixon appointees were referred to as a voting "bloc," a word faintly suggestive of unthinking and unfeeling cohesion. Despite the warnings of scholars that the "new appointees will not prove to be a solid predictable phalanx," the impression of a monolith persisted. "It is easy," remarked one observer, "to imagine Nixon thinking of them [his new appointees] as his Fearsome Foursome, mowing down the opposition of weak knees and bleeding hearts on the way to the goal line."[6]

It is not fair to say that all pictures of change were overdrawn or all fears of the Warren loyalists unfounded. Professor Paul Bender, of the University of Pennsylvania, feelingly expressed in *Harper's Magazine* the widespread misgiving that the advent of the Burger Court portended a repudiation of the Warren Court's chief mission:

> My fears for the future of the Court are these: for twenty years the Supreme Court not only decided important cases correctly but it also contributed enormously to an increasing sensitivity among many people in this country toward oppressive inequalities and injustices. . . . I'm not sure we would have come this far in our thinking without the Court to prod us and lead us. . . .
>
> It would be nothing short of tragic, however, if the result of the new Supreme Court were a spread of cynicism within the country toward persons who allege unfairness and injustice, and if we were to see a massive and abrupt closing of court doors in the face of litigants who have just begun to be aware that the law can, indeed, sometimes right the wrongs of the disliked and disadvantaged. I hope that doesn't happen.[7]

Earl Warren seemed to have been the personal embodiment of Bender's hopes; it may be impossible to understand fully the recent history of the Supreme Court without understanding the man himself. He had retired from the Court over two years before I clerked there, but I had met him at receptions in his honor and on occasion heard him speak. To me he looked the perfect grandfather, ruddy and healthy in advancing years, open and jovial by nature, a genial and tireless raconteur about years in politics and on the Court. He combined ease of manner and firmness of conviction to an exceptional degree. His view of law seemed so simple and straightforward, projecting the awesome strength of uncomplicated faith. He was, above all, humanitarian and egalitarian, and believed simply and boldly that law must treat men equally and not push down the nation's racial and ethnic minorities and the poor. When explaining landmark decisions, he was disarming and direct. The point of *Miranda,* he said, was that the state ought not to wait until trial to tell a man what rights he has, but rather inform him when the police first whisk him into custody, away from friends and home. *Baker* v. *Carr,* the decision that laid the groundwork for the Court's later one-man, one-vote requirement for state legislatures, was, he often contended, the most important in his time as Chief Justice. If the Court had long ago insisted all men have an equal right to vote, its later dramatic steps to correct racial injustice might never have been necessary.[8]

Opinions on the man will differ, just as they have on the Court he headed. But what precisely did the Supreme Court, in his sixteen years as Chief Justice, do? First and foremost, the Warren Court gave black Americans their first taste of equality after almost a century of limbo between technical emancipation and the full rights of citizenship. It gave them perhaps the first feeling that some branch of national government deeply and genuinely cared. Second, the Warren Court, by requiring state legislative districts of equal population, established the propriety of judicial intervention to ensure the fairness of ground rules under which elective combat was conducted. Third, the Court broadly expanded the panoply of constitutional protections for persons accused of crime. Finally, and more intangibly, the Warren Court brought a renaissance of judicial creativity, became the country's intellectual fountainhead of moral reform, and made the Supreme Court once again a force to be reckoned with in American life.

There was, I thought, much that was good in this contribution. The question I most often asked myself was whether the talk and auguries of change one heard everywhere really meant a deliberate destruction by the new Court of most of what Earl Warren stood for. I myself had never been a devout believer, but neither was I an indiscriminate leveler. One result of being a child of the 1960s, I suppose, is to ponder the moral implications and value of one's every experience. A wipeout of the Warren Court, as many feared, was not something I would have felt comfortable associating with, even in a law clerk's minor role.

One of Chief Justice Warren's earliest opinions was probably his most important: *Brown* v. *Board of Education,* where the Court ruled unanimously that state-imposed school segregation violated the Fourteenth Amendment of the United States Constitution, thereby setting in motion the modern movement for equal rights. Although *Brown* was afoot before Warren's predecessor, Chief Justice Frederick Vinson, departed the Court, it was Warren who wrote the opinion, helped create the unanimity, and personally bore much of the ensuing Southern anger. Although *Brown* alone would not rid the country of race consciousness and prejudice, it did say that as far as the law was concerned, blacks would henceforth be regarded as individuals and not as a separate and unwanted class. As an opinion, *Brown* was no model of scholarship or jurisprudence; in the eyes of its detractors it was sparse and conclusory, with a quick pass and a fast shuffle at some current social science. But its words were great ones because they spoke to a nation's conscience and heart:

> [T]he Court, in requiring that a Negro admitted to a white graduate school be treated like all other students, again resorted to intangible considerations: ". . . his ability to study, to engage in discussions and exchange views with other students, and, in general, to learn his profession." Such considerations apply with added force to children in grade and high schools. To separate them from others of similar age and qualifications solely because of their race generates a feeling of inferiority as to their status in the community that may affect their hearts and minds in a way unlikely ever to be undone.[9]

In the fall of 1973, almost two decades after *Brown*, I sat in a small restaurant with a friend who was quite studious and knowledgeable about the Supreme Court. He was also pessimistic. Already, the Burger Court's enthusiasm for racial justice seemed to be flagging. The Court had upheld the action of Jackson, Mississippi officials in closing municipal swimming pools in response to a federal desegregation order. It had refused the request of black and Mexican-American indigents to void a provision of the California constitution requiring popular approval in a local ref-

erendum before federally financed, low-income housing could be developed. It had given carte blanche to
discrimination in private clubs. Even *Swann* v. *Char-
lotte-Mecklenburg Board of Education,* where the Court
affirmed bus transportation of students as a permissible and sometimes necessary remedy for past state-
imposed public school segregation, was an opinion
whose backing and filling bespoke uneasy compromise among the Justices that could at any moment fly
apart. And in a sense, my friend continued, it already
had. The rule of unanimity in school desegregation
cases had broken in the 1971 term. (There the four
Nixon Justices had dissented from a Court holding
that establishment of a separate school system by the
town of Emporia, Virginia, would impede desegregation of the preexisting school district, comprised
jointly of Emporia and heavily black Greensville
County.)[10] Several Justices, he thought, had openly
rejected the bold steps still needed to achieve a genuinely integrated society. For some time, he concluded,
he had been fearful that the drive for racial equality
would die short of fruition. "The spirit of *Brown,*" he
said, "no longer resides at the Supreme Court."

His was easily the most damaging indictment that
could be made of the new Court. More than any other,
the challenge and test for America has been seen in an
honest solution to the race problem. And *Brown* had
made of the Supreme Court the nation's foremost
symbol of racial equality. For the Court to have initi-
ated expectations for racial justice and then to draw
back on them would be to send society into a hideous
and nightmarish backslide from which it would not
easily recover. *Brown* was the part of the Warren

legacy to be handled by the new Court with greatest care and was, so my friend contended, the foremost yardstick by which its humanitarian intentions would ultimately be judged.

I thought hard about my friend's words before replying. It seemed unfair to judge the Burger Court by the spirit of *Brown,* in much the same way, for example, as it would be unfair to compare the innovations and successes of the Truman domestic program with the standards of the New Deal. If the spirit of *Brown* no longer resided at the Supreme Court, it was not because the Court had exiled it, but because the conditions and complexion of the American race problem had fundamentally changed. Already *Brown* evoked in me a certain nostalgia, not because it was an easy step for the Court to take at the time, but because it was one of the last, great actions whose moral logic seemed so uncomplex and irrefutable, and whose opposition seemed so thoroughly extreme, rooted as it was in notions of racial hegemony and the constitutional premises of John C. Calhoun.

But *Brown* fought and won only the easiest part of the battle. It defeated segregation in its most visible and least defendable form, in the state statutes and constitutions of the South that bluntly and openly forbade white and black children to attend the same school. After *Brown* race prejudice became more discreet; discrimination no longer was embodied in state law but in the exercise of individual discretion. It is quite easy for the Constitution to void a state law or regulation that requires, to take an extreme example, policemen to give speeding tickets only to black drivers. It is inestimably more difficult for it to deal with an individual policeman who pulls mostly blacks to the side of the road. "Those I stopped were speeding," the policeman will inevitably say. Invariably, such "invisible" discrimination has some neutral nonracial justification. The policeman stops only speeders; the employer who hires only whites is seeking the best-qualified man; the restaurateur of a largely white establishment serves only those in coats and ties; the school board chairman of a predominantly segregated school district is seeking to preserve the values of neighborhood schools. Such justifications, if honestly applied, have great merit. But it is always very hard to tell in any given situation what in fact is afoot—the neutral justification or "invisible" race discrimination.

The law has not been particularly successful in answering this question, partly because it involves subtle assessments of human intentions and motivations. Determining whether a neutral justification or invisible discrimination is actually at work involves treacherous problems of legal proof.

The Warren Court ran against this problem in the 1965 case of *Swain* v. *Alabama.*[11] Prior to the trial of Swain, a Negro, the prosecutor of Talladega County, Alabama, struck all six Negroes from the petit jury venire, with the result that Swain was tried and convicted by an all-white jury. The question facing the Supreme Court was whether the actions of the prosecutor amounted to unconstitutional race discrimination. Here, inevitably, there was a neutral, nonracial justification for what the prosecutor had done. Prior to most American criminal trials, in an effort to get the fairest possible jury, both the state and the defense have traditionally been allowed a certain number of peremptory challenges of prospective jurors. And the peremptory challenges are quite often exercised on the most arbitrary grounds, because, for example, a lawyer does not like the way a prospective juror shifts his eyes or wears his hair. Any prosecutor would contend that he was not challenging Negroes as a race, but simply because some individual quirk of the prospective Negro jurors struck him as too oriented toward the defense. And was not this precisely the time-honored way in which peremptory challenges were understood to be exercised? Faced with this, the Supreme Court, over three dissenting votes, heavily backed the asserted, neutral justification and put on Swain an awesome burden to prove race discrimination. Swain not only had to show that no Negroes served on his particular jury but that virtually no Negroes had ever served as jurors in Talladega County, and, further, that the prosecutor was the one responsible for their exclusion.[12] The Court basically decided that the system of peremptory challenges to jurors was too valuable to an American trial to risk encumbering it with constitutional attacks. But, in so doing, it greatly facilitated "invisible" race discrimination in the choosing of Alabama jurymen.

Ironically, one of the Burger Court's maiden voyages into the neutral justification-invisible discrimination dilemma produced an opinion much more sympathetic to the black predicament than in *Swain*. The case, *Griggs* v. *Duke Power Co.*, concerned the vital area of minority employment.[13] After passage of the 1964 Civil Rights Act, employers could no longer announce openly a policy of whites-only hiring. But "invisible" discrimination soon began to appear. Some employers suddenly instituted standardized tests and educational requirements as a prerequisite for employment or advancement. These tests, justified as upgrading the quality of the employer's work force, also had the effect of reading many poorly educated black workers out of the job market. In judging the validity of such tests, however, the Court, in an opinion by Chief Justice Burger, took a different tack from *Swain* and placed the heavier burden of proof on the party asserting the neutral justification, in this case the employer. Recognizing that testing devices often operated as "built-in headwinds" for minority employment applicants, the Court insisted that "if an employment practice which operates to exclude Negroes cannot be shown to be related to job performance, the practice is prohibited." "History," advised the Chief Justice, "is filled with examples of men and women who rendered highly effective performance without the conventional badges of accomplishment in terms of certificates, diplomas, or degrees." One writer termed the opinion "a sensitive, liberal interpretation of title VII (of the 1964 Civil Rights Act). It has the imprimatur of permanence and may become a symbol of the Burger Court's concern for equal opportunity."[14]

The point is not to prove that the Burger Court is more or less liberal on matters of race. It has always been clear that the core of the Warren tradition—the prohibition of state-imposed segregation in public education and facilities and the support of congressional initiatives aimed at ending discrimination—remains firmly intact. But those are not generally the questions that reach the Supreme Court today. Rarely, in fact, does the race issue now appear in the context

of overt and easily detected prejudice or without
legitimate considerations on the other side. The Warren Court sensed this very early: the direction in 1955
to desegregate "with all deliberate speed" was as
much a product of diplomacy and compromise as any
language in the *Swann* opinion seventeen years later.
So too were the "sit-in" cases in the early 1960s where
the Warren Court struggled mightily with the question of Negro disruption and protests at segregated
lunch counters, bus stations, and statehouses of the
South, and finally, in *Adderly* v. *Florida,* came to feel
that the justice of black grievances did not override the
continued risk of legitimizing extralegal conduct.[15] Issues as hard as this and harder are pounding the
Burger Court. The ultimate question is whether opt-
ing on tempered occasion for the rule of law, a broad
scope for peremptory jury challenges or uniform
standards of employment, should somehow be viewed
as against the spirit of *Brown.* I did not believe so, and
thus answered my friend late that night that I could
not share his view that the spirit of *Brown* was now
dead.

If Warren Court protection of minorities and the
criminally suspect created public anger, its reapportionment decisions raised different resentments: those
of the legislative branch. For some time, elected office
holders had manipulated the ground rules of the political process with a sharp eye toward self-perpetuation.
In an effort to preserve incumbency and rural rule in
state legislatures, gross malapportionments had come
to exist: disparities between most and least heavily
populated legislative districts ran 242 to 1 in the Connecticut House, 223 to 1 in the Nevada Senate, 141 to

1 in the Rhode Island House, and 99 to 1 in the Georgia Senate. The hopes for legislative self-correction seemed dim. As Archibald Cox has noted: "If one arm of government cannot or will not solve an insistent problem, the pressure falls upon another." In *Baker* v. *Carr* and *Reynolds* v. *Sims,* the Supreme Court announced to the players in the political process that henceforth they had a referee.[16]

The Supreme Court has always ensured that the elective process respect the rights of free speech and dissent. And the Warren Court preserved and enlarged upon this tradition.[17] Its innovation was in holding that the ground rules of the contest—the election laws themselves—were now subject to court challenge. The poll tax was declared unconstitutional; the Georgia county unit system was abolished; state legislative and congressional districts and eventually those within local governing units were required to be equal in population.[18] The presence of the new referee angered those who had most profited under the old rules, namely elected incumbents. Senator Everett Dirksen found considerable support in Congress and among state lesislatures for his efforts to undo the Court's reapportionment rulings, efforts that faltered only because of the threat of filibuster and the difficulty of the constitutional amending process.

The purpose of the Supreme Court as political referee and its new one-man, one-vote rule was to make democratic election contests more representative. Toward the end of the Warren era, however, there were some indications that the referee was blowing the whistle too often, to the point of spoiling the game and frustrating the efforts of those trying to play. In

Kirkpatrick v. *Preisler* the Court struck down a maximum population deviation of 5.97 percent among Missouri's congressional districts and held that one-man, one-vote required a "good-faith effort to achieve precise mathematical equality" of population among congressional districts.[19] There was every reason to believe the ruling applied to state legislatures as well.

With the Warren Court's insistence on technical compliance with its rule, the referee kept on the players' backs, to the irritation of both. Continued friction between elected officials and the Court was unhealthy for the latter, whose authority and decisions depend ultimately upon public and political acceptance. The new quest for mathematical equality posed another danger also: "As a result [of the Court's rulings]," said political scientist Gordon Baker, "many have concluded that state legislatures now have a green light to gerrymander without constraints of existing county lines."[20] In other words, a smart politician, armed with slide rule, computer, map, and population tables for his state, could achieve the required mathematical equality of population, by moving bits of people here and there, all the while cutting county lines and the opposition to ribbons. That, says one astute political observer, is exactly what Nelson Rockefeller did to New York Democrats in 1971.[21]

In its first reapportionment decisions the Burger Court continued to act as referee, but became more tolerant of action on the field. In 1973 the Court held that apportionment plans containing up to 10 percent deviation in population between state legislative districts were presumptively valid and that somewhat larger deviations were permissible on the basis of some rational state policy, such as keeping an entire county or city within the same legislative district.[22] The decisions did not disturb the Warren Court's great contribution: the badly malapportioned legislatures of the early 1960s have been corrected and will remain so under the Court's new standards. Substantial equality of population remains apportionment's lodestar. But allowance of slight deviation as a matter of grace should keep Courts and state legislatures less in one another's hair and reduce pressure for the freakish gerrymander scurrying in and out of county lines to pick up precisely enough people. As *Washington Post* columnist David Broder observed on one recent reapportionment ruling:

> If Rehnquist, the most conservative of President Nixon's appointees to the Court, was now rewriting the one man–one vote doctrine over the dissent of the Warren court's remaining liberals —Justices Brennan, Douglas and Marshall—then it had to be bad news.
>
> Right? Wrong. At least, I think the quick conclusion is wrong. Rather, it seems to me that what Rehnquist's opinion has done is to rescue the court from the "arithmetic absolutism" into which it had drifted in its late 1960 applications of one man-one vote, and put the whole proposition of equality of representation back on a more sensible and defensible footing.[23]

More so than with desegregation and reapportionment, the Warren Court's protection of the criminal defendant has undergone change. Change had been expected, for the political mandate of the Burger Court was for a new direction in criminal rights or at least a halt to the old one. Even here, however, differences between the new Court and its predecessor may be less than popularly advertised.

Much of the Warren Court's revolution in the field of criminal rights may be traced to its suspicion of the major actors in the criminal process, state judges, prosecutors, and, above all, the police. The idea was that, left to their own devices, these parties could not be counted on to dispense justice to persons accused of crime. Despite our valued Bill of Rights, the history of American criminal justice has not been altogether an honorable one: stories exist, in the Supreme Court's own precedents, of a white sheriff and posse whipping and even hanging illiterate blacks to extort confessions.[24] By the time of the Warren era such extreme abuse and cruelty had mostly disappeared: that Court, however, remained sensitive to the subtler devices used by police and prosecutor to trap the accused and deprive him of exercise or even knowledge of rights granted him under the Constitution.

Given this basic skepticism, it became necessary for the Warren Court to keep police, prosecutors, and state judges under close watch and to build checks into the criminal-justice system to restrict their discretion. Thus police were required to give *Miranda* warnings to make sure stationhouse suspects knew their rights; they were further required, in a greater number of circumstances, to seek warrants from magistrates before they searched an office or home for incriminating evidence. Accused persons were provided lawyers in a great variety of situations to prevent police and prosecutors from putting them at a disadvantage. As for state judges, their decisions were made subject to lower federal court review as to any constitutional violation the accused might allege state authorities had worked upon him.[25]

The notion of checking the state's police and prosecuting power has always been important for America; the essence of individual liberty is that government not be able to punish the single citizen without good reason and strong proof. The very idea of trial by jury, for example, expresses our distrust of the state's awesome powers of confinement. But the Warren Court expanded this ancient theme of distrust in a revolutionary fashion. Traditionally, the main protections for persons accused of crime did not really apply until time for trial; the Warren Court pushed them forward to a suspect's first encounter with the police. Before the Warren Court the benefits of the Bill of Rights went mainly to those who could afford them; the Warren Court assaulted such distinctions of wealth and gave to destitute defendants lawyers and legal transcripts at public expense. Prior to the Warren era States had been free to disregard the stricter version of the Bill of Rights that applied to federal courts and federal law-enforcement officers. The Warren Court moved, step by step, toward a national Bill of Rights and forced state criminal machinery to comply.[26]

Such strides caused the most intense commotion. Many state and local governments balked at spending the money needed to administer the new rounds of hearings and pay the expenses of lawyers now due the accused. Police departments, accustomed to operating in their own way, resisted being put on tether by the

Court. "I'd have twenty guys in jail right now if we didn't have to operate under *present* search and seizure laws," was the typical comment of the head of the Minneapolis detective bureau.[27] If police and prosecutor detested Court interference with their business of securing convictions, many state judges saw Court decisions as impugning their capability and integrity. Thus, the Court's new rules created a built-in resistance on the part of those whose compliance with the rules was most necessary. When police and prosecutor ignored the rules in their search for evidence, courts responded by throwing out the evidence and often forfeiting convictions. The public outcry came, not against those who failed to follow the rules, but against those who formulated them. One of the Court's own members, Byron White, in his dissent to the *Miranda* decision set the tone: "In some unknown number of cases the Court's rule will return a killer, a rapist or other criminal to the streets and to the environment which produced him, to repeat his crime whenever it pleases him. As a consequence, there will not be a gain, but a loss, in human dignity."[28]

Today Justice White is not so often in dissent. He and the Nixon appointees, with the frequent help of Justice Stewart, are seen as forming a dependable majority for the state in most criminal cases. The question becomes, Where does the new majority wish to proceed?

The somewhat tawdry signal of a new and tougher line was the case of *Harris* v. *New York*.[29] Viven Harris was a twenty-three-year-old drug addict who had left high school after the tenth grade. At his jury trial Harris denied making the sales of heroin for which he was indicted. The prosecutor used to impeach this testimony incriminating statements Harris had earlier made to the police. But the statements suffered at least one serious infirmity: the police, in securing them, had failed to first warn Harris of his right to remain silent and to have an attorney.

The Court nonetheless held that use of the statements for impeachment was legitimate, purportedly to prevent perjury at trial. Despite its modest size and tone, Chief Justice Burger's opinion flew in the face of the chief symbol of Warren Court criminal jurisprudence, *Miranda* v. *Arizona.* It seems certain the Warren Court would never have rewarded the failure of police to warn suspects of their rights with admissible trial statements, for impeachment or any other purpose. But the Burger Court turned the tables and put the prosecutor in the driver's seat: the defendant could fail to testify and have the jury wonder at his lack of explanation or, if he took the stand, risk impeachment with statements taken from him in the absence of knowledge of his constitutional rights.

On the face of it, then, the basic operating assumptions of the new majority seem precisely opposite from those of the Warren years. The Court now appears more willing to assume good faith in the conduct of prosecutor and police and to allow them slowly to regain less molested governance of their own domains. Devices once placed by the Warren Court into the criminal-justice system to check their discretion are now seen as impediments to effective law enforcement. Police may obtain search warrants more easily now[30] and their powers to stop and frisk suspects on the street have been substantially broadened.[31] Police may also show photographs of a suspect to a witness and place him in a preindictment police lineup in the absence of his lawyer.[32] Grand juries have now become a more formidable instrument of investigation into suspect activity.[33] Under *Harris,* prosecutors may use to impeach an accused at trial confessions that police obtained without warning him of his right to remain silent and have an attorney. The state may also prosecute a man for an act on which he had previously been compelled to testify though, of course, the compelled testimony or any evidence derived from it may not be used.[34] The irony of this new license was illustrated in the wake of a recent Supreme Court decision further expanding police search and seizure powers. Rather than letting out the customary howl at a Supreme Court opinion, one police chief, Jerry Wilson of the District of Columbia, was actually trying to *reassure* the public that the new decision would not create dragnet police powers. Said Wilson: "The ordinary person walking or driving down the street has nothing to fear" from police response to the latest Court ruling.[35]

Inevitably, Supreme Court Justices defy predictability, including the Nixon appointees in the area of criminal rights. Two surprising Burger Court cases were *Argersinger* v. *Hamlin,* where seven Justices agreed that no person may be imprisoned, even for a misdemeanor, unless he was represented by a lawyer at his trial, and *Morrissey* v. *Brewer,* where the Court unanimously held that an individual must be granted a hearing before his parole can be taken away. The rulings meant much greater protection for indigent suspects and greater burdens on the states.[36] By implication, both cases refused to accept the good faith of public officials as adequate protection for an accused misdemeanant facing imprisonment or a wayward parolee. Both decisions further resolved the tension between creation of a new constitutional right and the burden on legal resources needed to staff it in favor of the right's creation, a primary characteristic of the Warren years. In fact, they were Burger Court decisions in the classic Warren Court style. Chief Justice Burger's words in the parole case sounded hauntingly like those of his predecessor, cutting through form to substance to extend sympathetically constitutional protections beyond the moment of trial:

> [T]he liberty of a parolee, although indeterminate, includes many of the core values of unqualified liberty and its termination inflicts a 'grievous loss' on the parolee and often on others. It is hardly useful any longer to try to deal with this problem in terms of whether the parolee's liberty is a 'right' or a 'privilege.' By whatever name, the liberty is valuable and must be seen as within the protection of the Fourteenth Amendment. Its termination calls for some orderly process, however informal.[37]

Criminal rights is probably the area of the Supreme Court's work that is most prone to emotional reaction, either one of sympathy for a disadvantaged suspect or of outrage at the perpetrator of a violent crime. As such, it may also be the part of the Court's work most susceptible to swings of the pendulum after a change of personnel. Given the recent, rapid turnover of seats on the High Bench, and the "law and order" criteria for the new appointees, perhaps it is noteworthy that the reaction against the Warren Court criminal decisions has not been even more severe. As yet, no significant Warren Court holdings have been directly overruled, a major feat for a Court that itself turned over many opinions of its predecessors.[38]

But if the landmark Warren decisions have not as yet been overruled, are they destined for slow, but just as certain extinction? No flat answer can be given. The Warren Court's quest for uniformity in the standard of state and federal criminal justice and for rich and poor has not been set back. With the exception of a ruling permitting states but not federal courts the use of less than unanimous jury verdicts, the Burger Court has recognized a single Bill of Rights. And the most important right for the poor in the modern criminal process—the right to a decent lawyer—has in one crucial instance been expanded.[39] A quite significant change has occurred in those Warren Court cases inhibiting police discretion in their hunt for evidence. The principal Burger Court criminal decisions, those broadening police search and seizure powers, the scope of grand jury investigations, and prosecutors' use of evidence once thought to be wrongly obtained, have primarily been directed toward freeing the hand of official crime detection. But that part of the Warren legacy encouraging a fair and honest verdict through legal representation and assistance to the accused has survived more handsomely. The synthesis of the new Court's efforts to encourage the official search and use of relevant evidence and the Warren Court's insistence that the accused have greater wherewithal to test that evidence, may restore to criminal justice a rather basic function: the more trustworthy determination of the innocence or guilt of those with whom our system of justice deals.

I often thought it unfair to be thinking of the Burger Court solely in terms of what it had or had not done to the Warren legacy. As years pass, the new Court will stamp its own unique mark on the great constitutional issues. And the issues may be quite different from those that dominated the 1950s and 1960s. When clerking I could not guess exactly what the overriding judicial question of the coming decade would be. But one clue, I thought, lay in what might loosely be termed the "new morality," the cry of different groups within the country to remove well-defined Victorian stigmas and roles.

The Burger Court has shown signs of reacting receptively. It has gone far toward removing from a child the legal stigma of illegitimacy. It has upheld the first few claims of sex discrimination presented to it, striking down an Idaho law giving men mandatory preferences over women in appointments to administer a deceased's estate, and voiding discrimination against servicewomen in the Air Force's distribution of fringe and dependency benefits.[40]

Impatience with Victorian ways helped bring to the Burger Court two of its toughest challenges. The results could not have been more different. In its obscenity decisions the Court sided with the past. States were given broad powers to suppress pornographic depictions of sexual behavior.[41] The decisions assumed that it is possible to say just what is pornographic and what is not, always a difficult task in matters of taste. In the abortion cases, however, the Supreme Court recognized the innate right of a woman to secure an abortion during the earlier stages of pregnancy. The bold step caused one observer to wonder "that an issue so deeply controversial in social and religious and political terms should be resolved by a court at all. For no other court, anywhere, would undertake to speak for a society on such an issue." Admirers of the decision hailed the Court for "moving the law out of the 19th Century." As the *Washington Post* noted: "The decision points out that the majority of the criminal abortion laws in effect in the states today derive from statutory changes enacted in the latter half of the 19th Century and that prior to that time, 'a woman enjoyed a substantially broader right to terminate a pregnancy than she does in most states today.' "[42]

With the primary exception of the obscenity question, the Warren Court did not face the breakup of Victorian morality so much as the demise of Jim Crow. And it is still too early to tell how the Burger Court will finally respond to "new morality" issues or whether the issues themselves will prove ephemeral and lack the sustaining moral substance of the drive for racial justice. But it is most interesting that the present Court in resolving these issues has borrowed extensively from the tools of Warren Court jurisprudence. Sex discrimination may soon topple under the same constitutional axe that felled Jim Crow; four members of the present Court have already said that laws making sex distinctions are "suspect" under the Constitution in much the same manner as those based on race. The abortion decision, recognizing explicitly the woman's right to privacy, leaned in spirit if not in doctrine on an earlier Warren Court decision, *Griswold* v. *Connecticut,* which held that a Connecticut statute banning the use of contraceptives by married couples invaded the privacy of the marital bedroom. And in the obscenity cases the Burger Court both embellished and rejected definitions of obscenity found in Warren Court opinions some years before.[43]

The more I thought, the less possible it became to analyze the new Court independently of its predecessor. Perhaps this was because of the bold quality of what the Warren Court had accomplished, perhaps because of the ubiquitous forecasts for a sharp about-face, perhaps because Earl Warren's ideals for the dispossessed remained a live issue after his departure. But perhaps it went further than that, to something embedded within the nature of law and the institution I worked for, something about the Supreme Court, even after a time of rapid turnover, that still made signs of continuity more prevalent than those of drastic change. Much more of the Warren legacy survived than was being destroyed. Not only was its work not being extinguished, the present Court was, in the main, working responsibly with that tradition, shaping and adapting it to new circumstances and problems.

Had I not felt this way, my time at the Supreme Court would have been less happy. It seemed important to make effort count for something in which one believes, not in every particular, but over the general course. My clerkship was gratifying for many reasons, but partly because the Supreme Court appeared to me to be working in the manner for which it was designed. That, contrary to popular portents of drastic dislocation, the new Court was balancing requirements of continuity with those of change.

The Supreme Court, I was convinced, is the most fascinating branch of American government. Lacking an elective mandate, the Court is perennially vulnerable; I have often wondered how it managed to survive. Beethoven's Fourth Symphony is a beautiful and serene piece between the more boisterous themes of the Third and Fifth. Schumann even called the symphony "a slender Greek maiden between two Norse giants."[44] That image might aptly describe the place in government of the United States Supreme Court.

Justice Douglas once said in a speech that "the voice of conscience is more compelling than the clamor of a mob."[45] The statement can as easily be thought to mean that the conscience of a Supreme Court Justice is more exalted than the wishes of the people of the country. That does not make Justice Douglas' statement illegitimate; it merely underscores the elitist edge of the Supreme Court's job. To take an example: the root causes of crime run deep, and Supreme Court decisions one way or another may not greatly change them. But the Supreme Court, in relation to the crime issue, is clearly the tip of the iceberg, and as the tip, its decisions are visible. To continue in the late 1960s its reversal of criminal convictions in the name of individual rights at a time of rising public concern over crime was an explosive course. Was such action the "voice of conscience" or a disdainful disregard of public opinion?

The Warren Court continually raised such questions about the Supreme Court as an institution. The irony of its decisions was apparent. Its purpose of revitalizing state government in the reapportionment cases may not square with the fact that through variously named constitutional doctrines and clauses such as preemption, incorporation, habeas corpus, and equal protection, the Warren Court stimulated the greatest drain of power from state to federal government since the New Deal. The enhancement of the democratic faith through one-man, one-vote put into question the activism of an "antidemocratic" institution such as the Supreme Court in other areas. The protection of blacks and indigent criminal suspects raised questions as to the relationship between a Supreme Court and majority welfare, as to whether any governing institution, in a democracy, could or should remain actively and permanently committed to minority causes.

The basic nature of the Constitution and Bill of Rights demands that the Supreme Court protect minorities of all sorts from political injustice. Yet the Supreme Court is purposely not put beyond range of political retribution, and there are and always have been distinctive limits to its powers. Not surprisingly, the leader of the Court's most activist era, Chief Justice Warren, all along claimed that the Supreme Court was essentially a passive institution:

> But the court is not a self-starter. . . . It can never reach out and grab any issue and bring it into the court and decide it, no matter how strongly it may feel about the condition it's confronted with. It is a creature of the litigation that is brought to it. . . . And so many people can't understand that, because they believe that a lot of

the people come there committed to a definite course of conduct and action depending upon their views, their political views. And they think if they see something they don't like, they just pull it into the court and decide it. But that is not true, the court is very limited in its jurisdiction.[46]

Warren's comments hit an important point: that whatever the lay of its decisions, the Court's strength lay in its continuance as a court and in an institutional posture of passive virtuosity. The passivity does not merely relate to the fact that the Supreme Court is a creature of the cases that come to it or that the Court may often prefer to decide those cases in the narrowest possible way. The passive virtues apply to the conduct of Justices as well.

Justices do not, as a rule, engage in public debate or offer gratuitous opinions on political issues or candidates; their public speeches very often have a bland and abstract ring. Such abstinence and nonpartisanship also extends to their clerks. Justice Powell tactfully let it be known that he did not want me to attend partisan political gatherings while working for him; he would have been disappointed had I, while a law clerk, so much as signed my name to a public petition.

At times a passive state is very difficult to maintain. One evening, on the radio news, I heard the following bulletin: "Today the Supreme Court ruled that police must get a search warrant in certain circumstances." The statement was not altogether inaccurate; it was just that what the radio said the Supreme Court was doing *today* had been true of its cases for almost the last hundred years. The bulletin bore almost no connection with the day's actual search and seizure case which had held that consent to a police search might be valid, even though the object of the search had not been warned by the police of his right to refuse such consent. The bulletin made me wonder. I was convinced that the Court, possibly because of the legal and technical nature of much of its business, was the most misinterpreted and misunderstood branch of government. Yet it did not, except in the rarest instances, reply to such misunderstanding or itself seek to correct it. It endured all sorts of distortion and malignment; and yet, the Justices stayed silent, relying, I suppose, upon friends and followers of the Court's work to set things straight. I could not imagine a Justice attacking the press, even in tones far more moderate than those of Spiro Agnew. The Supreme Court was, in many ways, a mute branch of government. I asked myself why.

Again the answer seemed that whatever the "political" tenor of its decisions, the Supreme Court must remain a court. That it must somehow seem to be above the give and take between the press and the political branches, or between the political branches themselves. Perhaps the key to its legitimacy and moral authority lay in a kind of institutional asceticism. Again the Beethoven analogy came to mind: amidst Congress and President, the Court must continue the "slender Greek maiden," pristine, pure, restrained, but with a certain elite and elegant touch. Or was it too late in the day to fool anybody? Was the Court, despite its whited veil, bruised from decades of hard and controversial political acts?

The fascination of the Supreme Court is that its true

nature is insolubly shrouded in paradox and ambiguity. One ambiguity pertains to the final judgment of the Court itself. Is it in reality a collective judgment or simply the product of nine autonomous decisions on the part of the individual Justices? It is something of both, and though the final result in a case represents the votes of nine separate individuals, that whole is something greater than its parts.

The judging process at the Supreme Court has its "collective" features; a question of a Justice at oral argument may have as much influence on a colleague as it does on the Justice asking it. Justices discuss cases together at conference and comment and request changes on one another's draft opinions. Exchanges among the Justices are about as free and open as busy schedules will permit. But though the Court's final decision is to this degree interpersonal, the office of each Justice is also a world unto itself, the nine "tombs" I used to think them, so separate and sealed off they sometimes seemed to be. Each Justice operates at his own pace and often makes up his own mind in a very private way. Each Justice's chambers carries its own particular focus of debate. And the constitutional issues that trouble one Justice may be less bothersome to another. A case, for example, that poses very serious questions in terms of Justice Stewart's view of the equal protection clause may be much easier for Justice Marshall, or vice versa. Justices Douglas' and Black's more absolute views of the First Amendment made many obscenity cases easier for them to resolve than for their colleagues. Thus, the collective decision on a case at the Supreme Court is made more intriguing by nine individual strategies and dramas taking place within each Justice's chambers. And the independence of each unit makes the Court resistant to lobbying or strong-arming on the part of a single, aggressive Justice. Though interpersonal discussion is seen as helpful in forming the Court's collegial judgment, aggressive personal lobbying for one's point of view is not. The line between persuasion and pressure is a subtle one, but one generally honored in the Court's etiquette.

The place of personal independence within the Supreme Court has somehow escaped those who see the Nixon Justices in lockstep. Perhaps interpretations of the Supreme Court will always present Justices in blocs, whether liberal, moderate, or conservative. The distinguished Yale Professor of History John Morton Blum used to refer disparagingly in his lectures to the four Justices who most doubted the constitutionality of New Deal reforms (Willis Van Devanter, James McReynolds, George Sutherland, and Pierce Butler) as the "four paleoliths," thus slighting the fact that at least one of the four, Justice Sutherland, had a brilliant, if rather theoretical, juristic mind. Chief Justice Warren and Justices Black, Douglas, Brennan, and Goldberg were called more times than I can remember the activist "bloc" or "wedge," overlooking the most enormous variants in individual styles and views. I understood why this was done. It is a convenient, sometimes necessary way of simplifying a complex institution and of having divisions on the Supreme Court more closely approximate the public perception of political combat. But that such expressions do violence to the Court's central ideal—that of decision reached through nine, independent judgments—is hardly ever noticed.

One recent Court clerk has written, "Now it may be inaccurate to deny that the Court is divided along clear factional lines, and into stable blocs."[47] Today's Supreme Court is indeed discussed in blocs, the inevitable consequence of a President making four appointments with an openly touted political purpose. Thus the Nixon "bloc" of Burger, Blackmun, Powell, and Rehnquist often stand together in the public spotlight. The most frequent public breakdown of the entire Court has the four Nixon Justices in one corner, three "liberal" Warren Court holdovers, Justices Marshall, Brennan, and Douglas, in another, with Justices Stewart and White in between. *Newsweek* reported that "some Court watchers think they see the beginnings of a new triple-troika pattern with Burger, Blackmun, and Rehnquist more or less predictably arrayed on one side, Douglas, Marshall and Brennan on the other —and Powell, Stewart, and White determining the outcome from their position in between."[48] Such bloc breakdowns of the Court rely heavily on statistical data showing, in essence, that Justice X voted with Justice Y a certain percentage of the time. The *Harvard Law Review,* which annually conducts the most thorough compilation of this data, found that in the 1971 term, for example, in forty-five of the seventy decisions in which all four Nixon appointees voted, they all joined in one opinion. With one insignificant exception, "each of the four Nixon Justices agreed with each of the other three Nixon Justices a higher percentage of the time than he agreed with any of the five non-Nixon

Justices." And by far the lowest percentage of agreements were recorded between the Nixon appointees and the three "liberal" Warren Court holdovers, Justices Douglas, Brennan, and Marshall.[49]

Yet the "bloc" and "faction" portraits of the United States Supreme Court have fatal drawbacks: they infer that Justices function in coalition rather than as individuals. Coalitions are, of course, a working principle of politics. They are loosely formed alliances of different groups in attempts to gain or hold power. The pressure for this sort of alliance is vastly reduced in a Supreme Court where Justices vote equally, hold office for life, and where most rules of operation are firmly and traditionally established. Often, coalitions imply mutual exchange of support on issues that have little, if any, relationship: in political terminology, log-rolling. The classic logroll is simple: the North Dakota Senator promises to resist closing a military base in Georgia for Georgia's support of appropriations to build a dam in North Dakota. On the Supreme Court the logroll would be a shocking breach of etiquette. One Justice does not suggest that a second Justice join his opinion in a case in return for the first Justice's vote in an unrelated case. In the Court, to be sure, a Justice desires that his views become those of a majority. But there exist no prearrangements, tacit or otherwise, that certain Justices will band together on certain issues to assure that majority.

The uniqueness of the Supreme Court lies in having nine independent judgments on the merits of each case, a uniqueness that the talk of blocs and tables of statistics successfully obscures. The fact that the four Nixon appointees or the three "liberals" voted the same way on a case does not mean they moved as a bloc. Opinions often represent precarious compromise of the differing views of those that joined them. Votes are more often independently reasoned than swayed. Where they are swayed, it is most often on the merits, not on the ground that "if Bill has done it, it must be O.K."

Grouping Justices into blocs implies indistinguishability, that Justices of a certain stripe are freely substitutable, that one "strict constructionist" or one "activist" is much the same as any other. But it does not take long, for example, to sense that Justice Douglas is a much different jurist from other members of the so-called "liberal" bloc on the present Court or, in fact, from any other "liberal" Justice, present or past. The difference is not that Justice Douglas takes twenty-mile hikes, authors books at a prolific pace, or recently has led his colleagues by a wide margin in the number of opinions written during a term. Nor is the difference solely that Justice Douglas is "liberal" and "activist" to a greater degree. Much of Douglas's uniqueness lies in his forging the words of the Constitution with a keen and vivid social vision. The vision is based on two words: freedom and equality. A virtually absolute freedom of speech and expression and the freedom of an individual to a private enclave of life, away from the state's intrusion and observance. The Justice, quiet and mild in his personal manner, has also in his thirty-five years on the Supreme Court been a rugged warrior for the underprivileged. His vision of a more egalitarian and libertarian society runs freely throughout his opinions, so vividly, in fact, as to seem more sociological than jurisprudential and to thrust upon him a degree of controversy, rare even for a Supreme Court Justice.

With true freedom, believes Douglas, comes a healthy tumult. As he wrote in defense of the right of Students for a Democratic Society (SDS) to recognition as a campus organization, despite opposition from the college administration:

> The present case is miniscule in the events of the 60s and 70s. But the fact that it has to come here for ultimate resolution indicates the sickness of our academic world, measured by First Amendment standards. Students as well as faculty are entitled to credentials in their search for truth. If we are to become an integrated, adult society, rather than a stubborn status quo opposed to change, students and faculties should have communal interests in which each age learns from the other. Without ferment of one kind or another, a college or university . . . becomes a useless appendage to a society which traditionally has reflected the spirit of rebellion.[50]

The request of the Nixon administration for authority to wiretap alleged threats to national security without a court order brought from Justice Douglas this sharp rebuke:

> [W]e are currently in the throes of another national seizure of paranoia, resembling the hysteria which surrounded the Alien and Sedition Acts, the Palmer Raids, and the McCarthy era. Those who register dissent or who petition their

governments for redress are subjected to scrutiny by grand juries, by the FBI, or even by the military. Their associates are interrogated. Their homes are bugged and their telephones are wiretapped. They are befriended by secret government informers. Their patriotism and loyalty are questioned. . . .

We have as much or more to fear from the erosion of our sense of privacy and independence by the omnipresent electronic ear of Government as we do from the likelihood that fomenters of domestic upheaval will modify our form of governing. (Footnotes omitted.)[51]

The Justice's fight for the dispossessed is best symbolized in his view of the public involvement necessary to invoke the Fourteenth Amendment guarantees:

I think it is time to state that there is no constitutional difference between *de jure* and *de facto* segregation, for each is the product of state actions or policies. If a 'neighborhood' or 'geographical' unit has been created along racial lines by reason of the play of restrictive covenants that restrict certain areas to 'the elite,' leaving 'the undesirables' to move elsewhere, there is state action in the constitutional sense because the force of law is placed behind those covenants.

There is state action in the constitutional sense when public funds are dispensed by urban government agencies to build racial ghettoes.

Where the school district is racially mixed and the races are segregated in separate schools,

where black teachers are assigned almost exclusively to black schools, where the school board
closed existing schools located in fringe areas
and built new schools in black areas and in distant
white areas, where the school board continued
the 'neighborhood' school policy at the elemen-
tary level, these actions constitute state action. . . .

The Constitution and Bill of Rights have described the design of a pluralistic society. The
individual has the right to seek such companions
as he desires. But a State is barred from creating
by one device or another ghettoes that determine
the school one is compelled to attend.[52]

Justice Douglas has agreed with Justices Marshall
and Brennan as often as he has with anyone. Yet it
hardly seems fitting to describe the three men as a
liberal bloc. Justice William Brennan, for example, has
kept a much lower public profile than Justice Douglas.
Yet he has been an elemental force for change, precisely because he stood at the vortex of practically all
of the Warren Court's most complex undertakings.
Through important opinions he took a leading hand
in the reapportionment cases and in many school
desegregation problems in the aftermath of *Brown*.[53]
Perhaps his most complex and controversial efforts
involved attempts to straighten out the thorny interre-
lationships between state and federal court systems
and the delicate First Amendment questions in obscenity censorship and libel suits.[54] Though he is
often termed a "liberal," the difficulty of Brennan's
labors owed partly to the fact that his view of constitu-

tional provisions has not been absolute; he has tried hard to pick a path between competing values. But his willingness to allow state government some room to regulate obscenity, to permit libel suits in the face of wanton irresponsibility on the part of the press, and to exempt such things as the blood tests, fingerprints, and photographs of a criminal suspect from the privilege against self-incrimination aroused sharp disagreement from Justices Black's and Douglas' more literal and absolute reading of constitutional provisions.[55] A warm and affable man, Justice Brennan's precise, lawyerly, often understated tone has worked to give the "liberal" constitutional faith the strongest intellectual and analytical base. That he and Douglas differ is no cause for lament: the expression of the "liberal" viewpoint on the Court is enriched through their complementing views and styles.

Though they are not often seen as members of a bloc or faction, Justices Stewart and White are frequently lumped together as the present Court's moderates or swing men. Yet it is the distinctions between them that go far toward explaining the post-Warren Supreme Court.

Their early backgrounds were quite different. White grew up in modest circumstances on the Colorado frontier and Stewart in the Taft Republican city of Cincinnati. White's ascension from the sugar-beet fields of his boyhood to Supreme Court Justice has been swift. He has harvested America's more glamorous badges: junior Phi Beta Kappa, Rhodes Scholar, Supreme Court clerk, college and professional football star, deputy Attorney General under President

Kennedy, and then, at forty-four, Associate Justice of the United States Supreme Court. A former clerk Lance Liebman described him this way:

> From his arrival in Boulder [University of Colorado] in 1934 until now, White has been meeting challenges, competing and succeeding. Each time, his performances have been graded highly, and he has been advanced to the next rung.
> These successes bred confidence not only in himself but also in the system that has rewarded him. Such rewards for responsibility developed commitment to the shouldering of responsibility by individuals, groups, and institutions.[56]

Liebman's portrait is of a tough-minded and pragmatic judge, deeply democratic in his faith and generously supportive of the efforts of the political process, especially at the federal level, to resolve a complex nation's problems. White, says Liebman, resists bold and sweeping statements of philosophy and equally eludes bold categorization of himself by others.

The categorization that falls especially wide of the mark is that of a hard-nosed Justice whose own self-reliance and self-discipline has somehow been translated into unswerving support of an American work ethic willing to allow those at the bottom of the barrel to "tough it out" against whatever obstacles they might encounter. If Justice White seems personally the paradigm of a self-made man, he has remained sensitive as a judge to laws that grind down the less fortunate. He has been, of course, less protective than

Warren Court majorities of those who would make
their way in disregard of law, and he has often sided
with the new Nixon appointees in rejecting further
restrictions on the activities of law enforcement. But
in many closely fought cases he has voted to enhance
the opportunities of disadvantaged groups: to remove
the legal stigma of illegitimacy, to make sex discrimination constitutionally suspect, to support the Negro's
plaint for equal justice.[57] His general disposition
seems to be that courts must remain sensitive to op-
pressive legal disabilities but not lightly excuse law-
breaking and wrongdoing on the part of those who
labor under them. In the important case of *San Antonio
Independent School District* v. *Rodriguez,* where the Court
upheld, against constitutional objections, disparities
in public school funds among Texas school districts,
White dissented. The parents of children in property-
poor districts, he felt, were incapable of better financing their own public schools.

> The difficulty with the Texas system . . . is that
> it provides a meaningful option to Alamo Heights
> and like school districts but almost none to Edge-
> wood and those other districts with a low per-
> pupil real estate tax base. In these latter districts,
> no matter how desirous parents are of supporting
> their schools with greater revenues, it is impossi-
> ble to do so through the use of the real estate
> property tax. In these districts the Texas system
> utterly fails to extend a realistic choice to parents
> because the property tax, which is the only reve-
> nue raising mechanism extended to school dis-
> tricts, is practically and legally unavailable. . . .[58]

In *Rodriguez* Justice Stewart belonged to the five-man majority. When questions of race were not involved, Justice Stewart has been more reluctant than Justice White to invalidate as a denial of "equal protection of the laws" state statutes and practices disadvantaging particular groups or depriving citizens of their so-called "fundamental rights." Personally, Justice Stewart found Texas' method of financing public schools "chaotic and unjust." Yet it did not, in his view, violate any substantive rights or liberties conferred by the Constitution. Nor was it for judges to use the vague words "equal protection of the laws" to try and create such rights where the Constitution had failed to do so.[59]

Justice Stewart's position in *Rodriguez* says much about him as a judge. He believes seriously in the Supreme Court as a court, in judges as legal officers, and in the judicial function as an important but carefully limited one. As with Justice White, he maintains respect for precedent and a willingness to accept Warren Court developments with which the two Justices initially disagreed. And Justice Stewart retains a strain of Harlanesque self-restraint that surfaced most directly in his tribute to one of the greatest self-restraining Justices, Robert Jackson:

> He [Jackson] saw that "judicial activism" could be a deadening and stultifying force. He knew that every coercive and centralizing court decision deals a blow, if sometimes only a little blow, first to the ability and then to the will of the democratic process to operate with responsibility and vigor. He understood, as only an experienced

advocate could understand, the shortcomings of
the adversary process as a substitute for the give-
and-take of informed self-government. He understood, as only a wise and sophisticated judge
could understand, how fallible the judges of even
a final court can be. He knew that the right answer to a problem of New York might not be the
right answer in North Dakota. He knew also that
there might be a better answer tomorrow than
the best of today's. He knew, in short, that the
great strength of the federal union our Constitution created lies in its capacity for self-innovation
and change.[60]

Yet some observers ironically see Justice Stewart as
something of a fourth "liberal" on the present Court.
Such political characterization overlooks the Justice's
starting inquiry: Does the Constitution itself grant the
right in question? Where Stewart has once found a
right constitutionally sanctioned, as for example the
historic rights of racial minorities under the Fourteenth Amendment,[61] he has defended it stoutly and,
in the process, reached progressive results. He has
supported constitutional protections for accused persons, but mainly *after* the initiation of judicial proceed-
ings, the point at which he believes many critical safeguards in the Bill of Rights come into play.[62] He
believes that the Fourth Amendment requires police,
as a rule, to obtain warrants before undertaking to
search for evidence, a requirement Stewart has
worked to uphold, sometimes over vigorous dissent
from Justice White.[63] He has befriended the First
Amendment right to free speech, not in the more ab-

solute sense of Justice Black, but as one of the Court's most skeptical scrutinizers of government justifications for inhibiting it. It is significant that in the 1971 term's most crucial free speech decisions—those involving the privilege of newsmen to withhold disclosure of confidential sources to grand juries, the rights of pamphleteers and handbillers at giant shopping centers, and the justiciability of Army surveillance of the political activities of individual civilians—Justice Stewart regarded as contrary to the First Amendment Court opinions written or joined by Justice White.[64]

Each Justice exhibits a distinctive opinion style. The best of Justice White's opinions seemed to me to reflect extensive research, scrupulous attention to fact, and a tenacious and oncoming logic that wraps around and about its subject. Also a tight reasoner, Justice Stewart has a particular talent for concise and lucid prose, enlivened by his occasional fondness for a sprightly phrase. When the Court upheld Congress' establishment of a fifty-dollar filing fee as a precondition to discharge in bankruptcy, Justice Stewart objected: "The Court today holds that Congress may say that some of the poor are too poor even to go bankrupt. I cannot agree." His dissent to one of the Court's less significant cases begins: "The only remarkable thing about this case is its presence in this Court." "The camel's nose is in the tent," he remarked in dismay to a Court ruling he saw opening the door to public regulation of the layout and makeup of a newspaper's pages. "This is the first such case, but I fear it may not be the last."[65]

Justice Stewart's stylistic gifts and phrasemaking flair may owe something to a yen for journalism, a

The Court

fraternity that, under the First Amendment, still commands his warm support. He reportedly once "toyed with the idea of a career in journalism after Henry R. Luce offered him a job at Time Inc."[66] At Yale he was editor of the campus newspaper, the *Yale Daily News*. The Justice in fact exemplified for me the best of old Yale, its graduates cultured and patrician, with a high and inbred social conscience, and saved in the end from stuffiness by a wonderful sense of camaraderie and wit.

The greatest recent temptation of Court watching has been to coin glib references to cohesion among the Nixon appointees. But if it seems dramatic to point to a bloc of four, the risks of oversimplification may be almost four times as great. Some observers have pointed to blocs within blocs. In the 1970 term, for example, Chief Justice Burger and Justice Blackmun joined the same opinion in 89.9 percent of the Court's decisions. The two men were further known to be close personal friends: Blackmun, in fact, was best man at Burger's wedding. They were both Minnesotans, and sports-oriented newsmen covering the Court dubbed them "the Minnesota Twins."

But the two are hardly judicial twins, anymore than Justices Brennan and Marshall were when, during the 1969 and 1968 terms, they joined the same opinion in 90.5 percent and 93.5 percent of the Court's decisions. The Chief Justice seems a gregarious figure, white haired, broad shouldered, of ambassadorial dash and ceremonial aplomb. Justice Blackmun is more reserved, quietly courteous, with a long reputation as a diligent and conscientious judge. His opinions are thorough, methodical, and meticulously

169

touch all bases (sometimes to the point of sequentially lettering or numbering every conceivable factor that influenced a decision).[67] The Chief Justice writes more as a committed advocate; his opinions move with verve; strong, even galvanizing statements; and imaginative, sometimes memorable, imagery. One William Baird had been convicted in Massachusetts of distributing vaginal foam to a woman of undetermined marital status after he had made a speech at Boston University. In *Eisenstadt* v. *Baird* the Supreme Court overturned the conviction on the ground that the Massachusetts statute impermissibly discriminated between married and unmarried persons in contraceptive distribution. The Chief Justice dissented vigorously and, at the end, colorfully:

> I am constrained to suggest that if the Constitution can be strained to invalidate the Massachusetts statute underlying appellee's conviction, we could quite as well employ it for the protection of a 'curbstone quack,' reminiscent of the 'medicine man' of times past, who attracted a crowd of the curious with a soapbox lecture and then plied them with free samples of some unproved remedy.[68]

Gerald Gunther has noted that while commentators could once accurately describe Chief Justice Burger and Justice Blackmun as the Minnesota Twins, "with every decision day it is becoming clearer that at least they are not Siamese ones."[69] The two have differed in significant instances, something a general voting statistic would not detect. Justice Blackmun dissented from a Court ruling, in which the Chief Justice joined, that California could require in its state constitution a referendum in any self-governing subdivision to approve development of federally financed low-income housing. Justice Blackmun found to violate constitutional requirements of church-state separation something the Chief Justice would have permitted: tuition reimbursement and state income-tax relief to parents of children attending parochial schools. And Justice Blackmun has been somewhat more willing than the Chief Justice to strike down state residency requirements as a condition of eligibility for voting and in-state university tuition rates.[70] In some major Court decisions Blackmun has joined in the Court's entire opinion, while the Chief Justice has concurred only in the Court's result.[71] One of the earliest and most significant disagreements between the two Justices concerned the question of whether the Sierra Club, a national environmental organization, possessed a sufficiently direct interest in the matter to seek a court injunction of Walt Disney Enterprises' construction of a thirty-five million-dollar ski resort in a portion of Sequoia National Forest. Chief Justice Burger joined in the Court's traditional answer that the Sierra Club lacked any such standing. Justice Blackmun, a dedicated conservationist, ended his dissent with a more universal view of each man's stake in the environment and a quotation from John Donne:

No man is an Iland, intire of itselfe; every man is a peece of the Continent, a part of the maine; if a Clod bee washed away by the Sea, Europe is the lesse, as well as if a Promontorie were, as well as

if a Mannor of thy friends or of thine owne were;
any man's death diminishes me, because I am
involved in Mankinde; And therefore never send
to know for whom the bell tolls; it tolls for thee.
(Devotions XVII)[72]

It is not clear as yet whether these individual differences forecast some basic distinctions in constitutional approach or simply an occasional willingness of
Justice Blackmun to vote a more centrist position in
noncriminal cases. The philosophies of the newest appointees have not as yet fully matured. Such things
take years of knowledge, reflection, and case experience at the Supreme Court level. As time passes, differences between the newest Justices may increase,
and distinctive constitutional approaches can be expected to emerge. As much as any man on the Court,
Justice Douglas has watched men and tides of opinion
come and go. Now, after thirty-five years of service, he
is the longest-sitting Justice in the Supreme Court's
history. As the Court's most activist "liberal," he
might have raised the alarum over the Court's recent
course. But a recent interview in *Time Magazine* caught
the veteran jurist in a more sanguine frame of mind:

The Court has never been comprised of stereo-
typed people. Now there are different men on the
Court, all of them honest and dedicated, but
dedicated to different parts of the Constitution.
That sort of shifting attention has been true from
the beginning of the Court, and it will always be
true. The shift has been overemphasized anyway.
Those who really study the cases will realize that

lately there is no solid bloc, no phalanx, no automatic lineup of certain people against others. It shifts on every type of case. We're all independent, we all got here under our own steam, and we're not subject to political or presidential pressure. And that's the way it works.[73]

I suppose everyone who has clerked at the Supreme Court wonders a little what small fragment of history he has watched and played a part in. I certainly did. In a way I was forced to. Much of what I read pictured the Supreme Court in sudden turnabout, wrought by a determined bloc of its newest members. The popular view was one of an institutional switch led by four faceless men. But while there I felt otherwise. Despite striking differences in the styles and views of each of the Justices, the Court as a whole continued pretty much on course. Obviously, there was adaptation and modification as new men faced new problems, and in the Court's scrutiny of law enforcement there has been some real change. But the genius of the place is that despite the popular picture of factional square-off and institutional about-face, appreciation of individual distinctiveness and institutional continuity remains the truer guide.

5

THE DEPARTURE

Suddenly, on June 28, 1973, I was no longer a law clerk. The job had for the past year and a half been so consuming that I had almost come to believe it was permanent as well. But just as a clerk feels indispensable, that his Justice and the Court might be worse off without him, he is quickly disabused. For it is time to leave: in a day he moves from the side of a Supreme Court Justice to being once again a recent law graduate on the beginning rungs of some long career. And the Court he leaves continues its disappointments and triumphs, much as it did while he was there.

I left with mixed emotions. I was, of course, pleased to have the pace of life ease a bit. Much of life unhappily bypasses today's young professionals, so caught up are we in work. But departing the Court was in one sense a return to the world of sunlight, with a chance to blink and stretch and stare around. Much of the summer after my clerkship I spent in travel, revisiting friends, and in private thoughts and readings.

Yet I was surprised at how soon I missed the Court and the sense of action and excitement that always seemed to be there. As a clerk, I had been able to watch the play develop, the strategy of an important case unfold, to witness some of the debate when it counted most—before the final decision had been made. Suddenly, I was reading about the Supreme Court in the *Washington Post* at the same time and in the same manner as any casual observer. I had always been sad to relinquish an inside perspective on any institution; it seemed much of the intimacy and belonging went as well. "Today, the Supreme Court voted . . .," the newspaper now read. Secondhand news often made me feel outcast.

I was grateful for what a Supreme Court clerkship meant in starting a legal career. But it also meant that more was expected from me, in much the same way it is often remarked of a Rhodes Scholar or a Phi Beta Kappa or a student-body president that they have a "brilliant future." Perhaps, deep personal recriminations would someday arise if the future failed to materialize. But whether I achieved the professional success the clerkship predicted was not now the chief point. For over a year, in my mid-twenties, I had been afforded firsthand insight and participation at the highest level of American government. How, I wondered, does anything in later life approximate such an opportunity? Perhaps it would not; life was nothing more than the sum of one's personal experiences, and for a moment I worried that one of the best already lay behind me.

Events moved much too fast for such thoughts to linger. In my last months as a clerk the question of what my next job might be quite concerned me. The problem for a clerk is not a lack of opportunity, but of making a decision. Several of my friends among the clerks joined law firms in places as diverse as San Francisco, Washington, D.C., Indianapolis, New York, Denver, and Jackson, Mississippi. Others joined the law faculties at the Universities of Iowa, Stanford, Yale, Chicago, Michigan, and Wisconsin. Still others took jobs with the Special Prosecutor's office, as legislative assistants to some United States Senator, as speech writers in upcoming political campaigns, or with the NAACP legal defense fund.

My own decision concerned whether to teach or practice law. Both paths appealed to me, but I finally chose teaching. My time as a clerk definitely influenced that decision. I had become deeply intrigued by the Supreme Court and constitutional decision making and wanted the opportunity to continue that interest. The chance to write, to stimulate thoughts in others, and to better control my own time and lifestyle also played a part in the decision to teach. From watching lawyers and political candidates I had come to believe that effective oral communication was a great challenge and an art. Teaching law, I hoped, might develop that to the utmost because law students, at least in theory, are not supposed to sit supinely by, but to question and challenge a professor's viewpoint.

By fall I was teaching law at the University of Virginia, where preparation of courses left little time to reflect. The clerkship proved invaluable to teaching: as a student, appellate opinions had seemed an abstraction, but after clerking they became more a product of real life. As a teacher, my problem was clear: how to communicate the Supreme Court as a human institution, a vital and responsive branch of government, not a set of disembodied ideas. There are manifold frustrations to any such attempt. The nature of Supreme Court decision is enormously complex and at the same time enormously vulnerable to oversimplification. Students, like many others, latch on to half truths and images without grasping their limitations. The Court is "political"; "they'll [the Justices] just do what they want to anyway," my students tell me, and teaching becomes a constant combat with ideas I had tried to wrestle through myself not long ago. Unqualified visions have a strong and vibrant place in the world of ideas, but, I argue, they do not generally suit the United States Supreme Court.

My first autumn teaching was also the autumn of Watergate. I watched the firing of Archibald Cox, the resignation of Elliot Richardson, the banishment of Spiro Agnew, the disappearance and incoherence of the tapes, the whole tragic sequence of dissemblance that diminished my respect for one administration and shook my faith in government to the core. I kept asking how much of what had happened was attributable to the bad judgment and propensities of one individual and how much was endemic to our political process, its secrecy and susceptibility to monied influence? For a while, that fall, there seemed little to look up to, or take pride in, or even to hope for. A stench had settled on Washington, long past the stage of quick or dramatic cure.

Often, during the unraveling scandal, I thought back on the Supreme Court. Its decisions were neither perfect nor ultimately knowledgeable, its Justices not always wise, its institutional future not problem-free. Yet the recollection reassured me. I felt relieved knowing personally that somewhere in government some institution carried on with an inner sense of its own integrity, a commitment to its public trust. That, as the man for whom I had worked believed, the nature of things might be what man has the will to make them.

NOTES

Chapter 1. The Acceptance

1. Interview with George C. Freeman, Jr., clerk to Justice Black in the 1956 term, *Richmond Times-Dispatch*, December 12, 1971.

2. Kurland, *1970 Term: Notes on the Emergence of the Burger Court*, 1971 SUP. CT. REV. 265, 320.

3. The President's speech was reprinted in *The New York Times*, October 22, 1971.

Chapter 2. The Clerk

1. Foundation of the Federal Bar Association, *Equal Justice Under Law, The Supreme Court in American Life* (Washington: National Geographic Society, 1965), p. 118.

2. Anthony Lewis, *Gideon's Trumpet* (New York: Alfred A. Knopf, 1964), p. 29.

3. Powell, "An Overburdened Supreme Court," Ad-

dress to the Fourth Circuit Judicial Conference, June 30, 1972.

4. The term "petitions for certiorari" is meant generally to cover all kinds of cases filed with the Supreme Court, including appeals. A fuller picture of the Court's case load each term may be found in the Annual Report, Director of the Administrative Office of U.S. Courts.

5. Brennan, "The National Court of Appeals: Another Dissent," Address to the First Circuit Judicial Conference, May 23, 1973, pp. 7 and 9. Washington *Post*, May 24, 1973.

6. The variations between the different chambers may be substantial. Justice Brennan has stated, for example, that "I try not to delegate any of the screening function to my law clerks and to do the complete task myself." In Brennan, "The National Court of Appeals," p. 6.

7. A. E. D. Howard and George Freeman, "Justice Hugo Black," interview in *Richmond Times-Dispatch,* December 12, 1971.

8. Harlan, "Manning the Dikes," Cardozo Lecture, October 28, 1958, Association of the Bar of the City of New York, p. 16.

9. Gideon v. Wainwright, 372 U.S. 335 (1963). Gideon's story has been superbly told in Anthony Lewis, *Gideon's Trumpet* (New York: Alfred A. Knopf, Inc., 1965).

10. See John P. MacKenzie, "Confession Case Reverses Usual Role," *Washington Post,* November 26, 1972.

11. For the description of Woodville, Mississippi, the author is indebted to Jack Nelson, "Supreme

Court to Rule on Mississippi Shootout," Los Angeles *Times*, January 17, 1973.

12. Various accounts of the events in Woodville may be found in MacKenzie, *supra*, note 10; Nelson, *supra*, note 11; and in the opinion in Chambers v. Mississippi, 410 U.S. 284 (1973).

13. MacKenzie, *supra*, note 10.

14. Chambers v. Mississippi, 410 U.S. 284, 302 (1973).

15. *Criminal Law Reporter*, 12 (February 28, 1973), 1082.

16. MacKenzie, *supra*, note 10.

17. Nelson, *supra*, note 11.

18. Weber v. Aetna Casualty & Surety Co., 406 U.S. 164 (1972).

19. San Antonio Independent School District v. Rodriguez, 411 U.S. 1 (1973).

20. James v. Strange, 407 U.S. 128 (1972).

21. In re Griffiths, 413 U.S. 717 (1973).

22. Harlan, *The Role of Oral Argument*, 41 CORNELL L. Q. 6 (1955).

23. 347 U.S. 483 (1954).

24. The Court began to reach the question in Green v. County School Board, 391 U.S. 430 (1968).

25. Linda Mathews, "Supreme Court Clerks: Fame in a Footnote," Los Angeles *Times*, January 5, 1972.

26. *Id.*

27. Various descriptions of the conference, on which this account is based, may be found in writings of retired or present Justices, see, for example, Tom C. Clark, *Inside the Court*, 19 FEDERAL RULES DECISIONS 303–310 (1956); William J. Brennan, *State Court Decisions and the Supreme Court*, 34 FLA. BAR J. 269 (1960);

see also "The Supreme Court: Deciding Whether to Decide," *Time Magazine,* December 11, 1972.

28. Brennan, *supra,* note 27, p. 273.

29. Clark, *supra,* note 27, p. 306.

30. *Id.,* p. 307.

31. December 11, 1972.

32. The historical material on law clerks is collected in Newland, *Personal Assistants to Supreme Court Justices: The Law Clerks,* 40. ORE. L. REV. 299 (1961). (The quote from Justice McReynolds, p. 306.)

33. *Mr. Justice Brandeis,* 70 HARV. L. REV. 769 (1957).

34. *The Evolution of a Judicial Philosophy: Selected Opinions and Papers of Justice John M. Harlan,* (Cambridge: Harvard University Press, 1969).

35. 76 HARV. L. REV. 673 (1963).

36. See, for example, Alan M. Dershowitz and John Hart Ely (former clerks to Justices Goldberg and Fortas, respectively), *Harris v. New York: Some Anxious Observations on the Candor and Logic of the Emerging Nixon Majority,* 80 YALE L. J. 1198 (1971).

37. *Report of the Study Group on the Caseload of the Supreme Court* (1972).

38. *New Republic,* February 17, 1973, and March 3, 1973.

39. The selection preferences are reported in Newland, *supra,* note 32, pp. 308–9. The quotation is from Baier, *The Law Clerks: Profile of an Institution,* 26 VAND. L. REV. 1125, 1139 (1973). Professor Baier's article introduces an illuminating symposium on the use of law clerks throughout the nation's courts in the November 1973 issue of the *Vanderbilt Law Review.*

40. "Who Writes Decisions of the Supreme Court?," December 13, 1957, and February 21, 1958.

A reply to Mr. Rehnquist, by William D. Rogers, "Do Law Clerks Wield Power in Supreme Court Cases?" is also in the February 21 issue.

41. Robert H. Jackson, *The Supreme Court in the American System of Government*, (Cambridge: Harvard University Press, 1955), p. 20.

42. *Id.*

43. Goldberg, "One Supreme Court," *New Republic*, February 10, 1973.

44. Bickel, "The Court: An Indictment Analyzed," *The New York Times Sunday Magazine*, April 27, 1958.

45. Howard, *supra*, note 8.

46. *Washington Star*, April 21, 1973.

Chapter 3. The Justice

1. *Richmond Times-Dispatch*, July 17, 1972.

2. "Impressions of a New Justice," *Report of the Virginia Bar Association*, 1972, p. 219.

3. *Id.*, p. 220.

4. *Id.*

5. *Id.*, pp. 221–2; *Richmond Times-Dispatch*, July 17, 1972.

6. Roe v. Wade, 410 U.S. 113 (1973).

7. 413 U.S. 189 (1973).

8. Jencks, "Busing—The Supreme Court Goes to the North," *The New York Times Sunday Magazine*, November 19, 1972, p. 41.

9. Keyes v. Denver School District, 413 U.S. 219 (1973). (Powell, J., concurring in part and dissenting in part).

10. *Id.*, p. 253.

11. *Richmond News Leader*, October 22, 1971.

12. Transcript of United Virginia Bankshares, Inc., testimonial dinner for the Honorable Lewis F. Powell, Jr., December 16, 1971, pp. 10–11.

13. *Tidewater Oil Co.* v. *United States,* 409 U.S. 151, 174, 177 (1972) (Douglas, J., dissenting).

14. See Brennan, "The National Court of Appeals: Another Dissent," Address to the First Circuit Judicial Conference, May 23, 1973.

15. See, for example, Address to the Fifth Circuit Judicial Conference, April 11, 1973, p. 12.

16. "An Overburdened Supreme Court," Address to the Fourth Circuit Judicial Conference, June 30, 1972, pp. 11–12.

17. Although the Court, of course, decides nonconstitutional questions, "the heart and spirit of the Supreme Court lie in its constitutional role." Powell, Address to the Fourth Circuit Judicial Conference, June 30, 1972, p. 9.

18. United States v. United States District Court, 407 U.S. 297 (1972).

19. Barker v. Wingo, 407 U.S. 514 (1972).

20. Kastigar v. United States, 406 U.S. 441 (1972).

21. Lloyd Corp. v. Tanner, 407 U.S. 551 (1972).

22. Healy v. James, 408 U.S. 169 (1972).

23. *New Republic,* June 10, 1972, p. 12.

24. *Washington Evening Star,* May 26, 1972.

25. *The New York Times,* July 2, 1972.

26. Gunther, *In Search of Judicial Quality on a Changing Court: The Case of Justice Powell,* 24 STANFORD L. REV., 1001, 1002 (1972).

27. Quoted in Lewis, *Gideon's Trumpet,* p. 80.

28. Los Angeles *Times,* January 5, 1972.

29. Meador, *Justice Black and His Law Clerks,* 15 ALA. L. REV. 57, 59–60 (1962).

30. Quoted from Freund, *On Understanding the Supreme Court* (Boston: Little, Brown and Co., 1949), p. 3.

31. *Id.*

32. Alexis de Tocqueville, *Democracy in America,* (P. Bradley ed., New York: Alfred A. Knopf, Inc., 1945), p. 280.

33. Oaks, *Legal History in the High Court—Habeas Corpus,* 64 MICH. L. REV. 451 (1966).

34. See the summary of Michigan Law School Professor Yale Kamisar's remarks quoted in James F. Simon, *In His Own Image* (New York: David McKay Co., 1973), p. 265.

35. Uviller, *Barker v. Wingo: Speedy Trial Gets a Fast Shuffle,* 72 COL. L. REV. 1376 (1972).

36. Wechsler, *Toward Neutral Principles of Constitutional Law,* 73 HARV. L. REV. 1, 15 (1959).

37. Transcript of UVB Inc. testimonial dinner, *supra,* note 12, p. 5.

38. Howard, *Mr. Justice Powell and the Emerging Nixon Majority,* 70 MICH. L. REV. 445 (1972).

39. Gunther, *supra,* note 26, p. 1014.

40. *Newsweek,* October 15, 1973, p. 26.

41. *Richmond Times-Dispatch,* August 1, 1971.

42. Quoted in Alpheus Mason, *The Supreme Court from Taft to Warren* (Baton Rouge: Louisiana State University Press, 1958), p. 192.

43. United States v. United States District Court, 407 U.S. 297, 314 (1972).

44. Prayer Breakfast Speech to American Bar Asso-

ciation, August 13, 1972, pp. 10–11. Excerpts from the speech were reported in *U.S. News & World Report,* August 28, 1972.

45. Powell, *A Lawyer Looks at Civil Disobedience,* 23 WASH. & LEE L. REV. 205, 206, 221, 230 (1966).

46. Prayer Breakfast Speech, *supra,* note 44, p. 5.

47. *Id.,* pp. 2–3.

48. Keyes v. Denver School District, 413 U.S. 246 (1973).

49. *Richmond Times-Dispatch,* December 7, 1971.

50. *Hearings on Nominations of William H. Rehnquist, of Arizona, and Lewis F. Powell, Jr., of Virginia, to be Associate Justices of the Supreme Court of the United States Before the Senate Committee on the Judiciary,* 92d Cong., 1st Sess., 1971, p. 285.

51. In re Griffiths, 413 U.S. 717 (1973).

52. Weber v. Aetna Casualty & Surety, 406 U.S. 164 (1972).

53. Chambers v. Mississippi, 410 U.S. 284 (1973).

54. James v. Strange, 407 U.S. 128, 136 (1972).

55. Transcript of UVB Inc. testimonial dinner, *supra,* note 12, p. 5.

56. *Richmond Times-Dispatch,* July 17, 1972.

57. Howard, *supra,* note 38, p. 449.

58. *Hearings, supra,* note 50, p. 219.

59. Statement of William B. Spong, then United States Senator from Virginia. *Hearings, supra,* note 50, p. 89.

60. Memorial to John Stewart Battle, *Report of the Virginia Bar Association,* 1972, pp. 291–2.

Chapter 4. The Court

1. Quoted from James Simon, *In His Own Image: The Supreme Court in Richard Nixon's America* (New York: David McKay Co., 1973), pp. 6–7.

2. *Time,* June 5, 1972; *Newsweek,* June 5, 1972; Graham, *The New York Times,* July 2, 1972; MacKenzie, *Washington Post,* January 20, 1973; Denniston, *Washington Evening Star,* May 23, 1972.

3. See Howard, *Mr. Justice Powell and the Emerging Nixon Majority,* 70 MICH. L. REV. 445 (1972); Dershowitz and Ely, *Harris v. New York: Some Anxious Observations on the Candor and Logic of the Emerging Nixon Majority,* 80 YALE L. J. 1198 (1971); Kurland, *1970 Term: Notes on the Emergence of the Burger Court,* 1971 SUP. CT. REV. 265.

4. "An Optimistic Appraisal: The Supreme Court's '71–'72 Term," *Civil Liberties,* October 1972, p. 1.

5. "Law and the 'Burger-Nixon' Court," *The New York Times,* August 9, 1972.

6. *New Republic,* July 15, 1972; the scholar's warning is Gunther's, *supra,* note 5, p. 37; Zelnick, "Whizzer White and the Fearsome Foursome," *Washington Monthly,* December 1972, p. 46.

7. "The Techniques of Subtle Erosion," *Harper's Magazine,* December 1972, p. 30.

8. See *The New York Times,* December 20, 1972, p. 43.

9. 347 U.S. 483, 493–4 (1954).

10. Palmer v. Thompson, 403 U.S. 217 (1971) (the pool-closing decision); James v. Valtierra, 402 U.S. 137 (1971) (the housing referendum decision). In Moose Lodge No. 107 v. Irvis, 407 U.S. 163 (1972)

(the private-club decision) the Court held that the grant of a state liquor license to a private club and its consequent regulation by the state liquor control board did not constitute sufficient public involvement under the Fourteenth Amendment to compel the club to change its segregated guest and membership policies. The *Swann* opinion may be found in 402 U.S. 1 (1971). The Emporia school case is Wright v. City of Emporia, 407 U.S. 451 (1972).

11. 380 U.S. 202 (1965).

12. 380 U.S. at 222–228. The dissenters were Chief Justice Warren and Justices Douglas and Goldberg. They would have held that the absence of qualified Negroes on Talladega County juries would alone make out a prima facie case of discrimination on the part of the state, without any defendant obligation to show prosecutorial responsibility.

13. Griggs v. Duke Power Co., 401 U.S. 424 (1971). Justices Powell and Rehnquist were not on the Court at the time of this decision. The principles of *Griggs* were largely reaffirmed, however, in Justice Powell's subsequent unanimous opinion, McDonnell Douglas v. Green, 411 U.S. 792 (1973).

14. Quotations from the Chief Justice's opinion are at 401 U.S. 431–3. The comment on *Griggs* is from Blumrosen, *Strangers in Paradise: Griggs v. Duke Power Co. and the Concept of Employment Discrimination,* 71 MICH. L. REV. 59, 63 (1972).

15. The phrase "all deliberate speed" is from Brown v. Board of Education, 349 U.S. 294, 301 (1955). Adderly v. Florida, 385 U.S. 39 (1966).

16. The malapportionment statistics are taken from "Congress and the Nation 1945–1964," *Congressional*

Quarterly Service (1965), p. 1525. The Cox quotation is from his book *The Warren Court, Constitutional Decision as an Instrument of Reform* (Cambridge: Harvard University Press, 1968), p. 118. Baker v. Carr, 369 U.S. 186 (1962); Reynolds v. Sims, 377 U.S. 533 (1964).

17. See especially New York Times Co. v. Sullivan, 376 U.S. 254 (1964), NAACP v. Alabama, 357 U.S. 449 (1958).

18. Gray v. Sanders, 372 U.S. 368 (1963) (the Georgia county unit case); Reynolds v. Sims, 377 U.S. 533 (1964) (decision mandating equality of population among state legislative districts); Wesberry v. Sanders, 376 U.S. 1 (1964) (decision requiring populational equality for congressional districts). Avery v. Midland County, 390 U.S. 474 (1968), is the lead case for one man, one vote at the local governing level. See also Hadley v. Junior College Dist., 397 U.S. 50 (1970).

19. 394 U.S. 526, 530–1 (1969). *Kirkpatrick's* applicability to state legislatures is well discussed in *The Supreme Court, 1972 Term*, 87 HARV. L. REV. 89, note 35 (1973).

20. Baker, "Gerrymandering: Privileged Sanctuary or Next Judicial Target," in *Reapportionment in the 1970s*, Nelson Polsby, ed., (Berkeley: University of California Press, 1971), p. 135.

21. Broder, " 'Absolute Arithmetic' and the Court," *Washington Post*, March 11, 1973.

22. Gaffney v. Cummings, 412 U.S. 735 (1973); White v. Regester, 412 U.S. 755 (1973); Mahan v. Howell, 410 U.S. 315 (1973). The *Kirkpatrick* rule still applies, however, to congressional districting. White v. Weiser, 412 U.S. 783 (1973).

23. Broder, *supra*, note 21.

24. See, for example, Brown v. Mississippi, 297 U.S. 278 (1936).

25. For a major contraction of police power to conduct warrantless searches, see Chimel v. California, 395 U.S. 752 (1969). Warrants themselves were made more difficult for police officers to obtain: Giordenello v. United States, 357 U.S. 480 (1958); Aguilar v. Texas, 378 U.S. 108 (1964); Spinelli v. United States, 393 U.S. 410 (1969). The major "right to counsel" decisions of the Warren Court are Gideon v. Wainwright, 372 U.S. 335 (1963) (for indigent state-felony defendants); Douglas v. California, 372 U.S. 353 (1963) (for first appeal); Mempa v. Rhay, 389 U.S. 129 (1967) (for sentencing, where sentencing has been deferred subject to probation); Coleman v. Alabama, 399 U.S. 1 (1970) (at a preliminary hearing). Although the principle of federal-court review of constitutional infirmities in state convictions was established shortly before the Warren era in Brown v. Allen, 344 U.S. 443 (1953), the scope of such review was significantly expanded in the Warren years: Townsend v. Sain, 372 U.S. 293 (1963); Fay v. Noia, 372 U.S. 391 (1963); see also Sanders v. United States, 373 U.S. 1 (1963); Kaufman v. United States, 394 U.S. 217 (1969).

26. Major cases for the Bill of Rights application to early police-suspect confrontation are Escobedo v. Illinois, 378 U.S. 478 (1964), Miranda v. Arizona, 384 U.S. 436 (1966), and United States v. Wade, 388 U.S. 218 (1967). Early lead cases establishing benefits for indigents in the criminal process are Griffin v. Illinois, 351 U.S. 12 (1956) (free transcript for indigents on appeal), Gideon v. Wainwright, 372 U.S. 335 (1963),

and Douglas v. California, 372 U.S. 353 (1963) (see note 25, *supra*). Warren Court application of provisions of the Bill of Rights to the states occurred principally in Mapp v. Ohio, 367 U.S. 643 (1961), Gideon v. Wainwright, *supra*, Malloy v. Hogan, 378 U.S. 1 (1964), Pointer v. Texas, 380 U.S. 400 (1965), Klopfer v. North Carolina, 386 U.S. 213 (1967), and Washington v. Texas, 388 U.S. 14 (1967).

27. Quoted in Kamisar, *On the Tactics of Police-Prosecution Oriented Critics of the Courts,* 49 CORNELL L. Q. 436, 442 (1964).

28. Miranda v. Arizona, 384 U.S. 436, 542 (White, J., dissenting).

29. 401 U.S. 222 (1971).

30. United States v. Harris, 403 U.S. 573 (1971).

31. Adams v. Williams, 407 U.S. 143 (1972).

32. United States v. Ash, 413 U.S. 300 (1973), and Kirby v. Illinois, 406 U.S. 682 (1972).

33. United States v. Dionisio, 410 U.S. 1 (1973); United States v. Calandra,—— U.S. —— (1974).

34. Kastigar v. United States, 406 U.S. 441 (1972).

35. *Washington Post,* December 12, 1973. The decision was United States v. Robinson, —— U.S. —— (1973).

36. Argersinger v. Hamlin, 407 U.S. 25 (1972); Morrissey v. Brewer, 408 U.S. 471 (1972).

37. 408 U.S. at 482.

38. See, for example, Mapp v. Ohio, 367 U.S. 643 (1961), overruling Wolf v. Colorado, 338 U.S. 25 (1949); Gideon v. Wainwright, 372 U.S. 335 (1963), overruling Betts v. Brady, 316 U.S. 455 (1942); Bruton v. United States, 391 U.S. 123 (1968), overruling Delli Paoli v. United States, 352 U.S. 232 (1957).

39. The jury-verdict cases are Johnson v. Louisiana, 406 U.S. 356 (1972), and Apodaca v. Oregon, 406 U.S. 404 (1972). The dual standard for state and federal courts is primarily the result of Justice Powell's concurring opinions, 406 U.S. at 366. The expansion of the right to counsel came in Argersinger v. Hamlin, discussed earlier. On the other hand, see Kirby v. Illinois and United States v. Ash, *supra*, note 32.

40. Weber v. Aetna Casualty & Surety Co., 406 U.S. 164 (1972) (the illegitimacy case); Reed v. Reed, 404 U.S. 71 (1971) (the estate case); Frontiero v. Richardson, 411 U.S. 677 (1973) (the Air Force benefits case).

41. See particularly Miller v. California, 413 U.S. 15 (1973), and Paris Adult Theatre I v. Slayton, 413 U.S. 49 (1973).

42. The abortion cases are Roe v. Wade, 410 U.S. 113 (1973), and Doe v. Bolton, 410 U.S. 179 (1973). The first quotation is that of Anthony Lewis, "Liberty, New and Old," *The New York Times*, February 3, 1973, p. 29. The *Post* quotation is from the editorial "Abortion: Out of the 19th Century," January 31, 1973.

43. Justices Brennan, Douglas, Marshall, and White would hold sex a "suspect" classification in Frontiero v. Richardson, *supra*, note 40. Griswold v. Connecticut, 381 U.S. 479 (1965), found the right of privacy in the "penumbras" to the Bill of Rights, whereas the abortion decisions found it in the Fourteenth Amendment's due process clause. The definition embellished was that of Roth v. United States, 354 U.S. 476 (1957), and that rejected is the view of the plurality in Memoirs v. Massachusetts, 383 U.S. 413 (1966).

44. From Charles Burr's notes to the Bruno Walter recording of Beethoven, Symphony No. 4 in B-Flat

Major, Op. 60 (Columbia, MS6055).

45. Douglas, "The Attack on the Accusatorial Systems," *Washington State Bar News* 26, nos. 8–9, p. 5.

46. "The Talk of Chief Justices, Past and Present," *The New York Times,* December 20, 1972. Warren's observations are reported from a talk with Abram Sachar, Chancellor of Brandeis University, on WGBH Boston and the Public Broadcasting Service.

47. Liebman, "Swing Man on the Supreme Court," *The New York Times Sunday Magazine,* October 8, 1972, p. 16. Liebman clerked for Justice Byron R. White from 1967 to 1968.

48. *Newsweek,* October 15, 1973, pp. 24–25.

49. See 86 Harv. L. Rev. 297–302 (1972). The quotation is from p. 297.

50. Healy v. James, 408 U.S. 169, 197 (1972) (opinion of Douglas, J.).

51. United States v. United States District Court, 407 U.S. 297, 329–31, 333 (1972) (Douglas, J., concurring).

52. Keyes v. Denver School District, 412 U.S. 189, 216 (1973) (Douglas J.).

53. See, for example, Baker v. Carr, 369 U.S. 186 (1962), and Kirkpatrick v. Preisler, 394 U.S. 526 (1969), in the reapportionment area and Green v. County School Board, 391 U.S. 430 (1968), and Keyes v. Denver School District, 413 U.S. 189 (1973), in the school desegregation field, the latter, of course, a post-Warren Court opinion.

54. For federal-state court relationships, see especially Fay v. Noia, 372 U.S. 391 (1963); for obscenity, Roth v. United States, 354 U.S. 476 (1957), and Memoirs v. Massachusetts, 383 U.S. 413 (1966) (plurality

opinion); and for libel, see New York Times Co. v. Sullivan, 376 U.S. 254 (1964).

55. See Roth v. United States, 354 U.S. 476, 508 (Douglas, J., with whom Black joins, dissenting); New York Times Co. v. Sullivan, 376 U.S. 254, 293 (Black, J., with whom Douglas joins, concurring); Schmerber v. California, 384 U.S. 757, 773 (Black, J., with whom Douglas joins, dissenting). Differences, though of lesser scope, continued between Justices Brennan and Douglas on the obscenity question after the latest opinions. Compare Paris Adult Theatre I v. Slayton, 413 U.S. 49, 73 (1973) (Brennan, J., dissenting), with Miller v. California, 413 U.S. 15, 37 (1973) (Douglas, J., dissenting).

56. Liebman, *supra,* note 47, p. 17.

57. See Levy v. Louisiana, 391 U.S. 68 (1968), Labine v. Vincent, 401 U.S. 532 (1971), Weber v. Aetna Casualty & Surety Co., 406 U.S. 164 (1972), all illegitimacy cases; Frontiero v. Richardson, 411 U.S. 677 (1973) (the sex-discrimination case); and Reitman v. Mulkey, 387 U.S. 369 (1967), Palmer v. Thompson, 403 U.S. 217 (1971), Wright v. City of Emporia, 407 U.S. 451 (1972), all civil rights cases. With the exception of *Weber,* the Justices' positions in these cases were closely divided, either by 5–4 or 6–3 margins. In *Labine* and *Palmer* White's votes in behalf of black and illegitimate plaintiffs were in dissent.

58. San Antonio Independent School District v. Rodriguez, 411 U.S. 1, 64 (1973) (White, J., dissenting).

59. *Id.,* pp. 59–62 (Stewart, J., concurring).

60. Quoted in Simon, *supra,* note 1, pp. 178–9.

61. The Justice has also apparently accepted those

"other classifications that, at least in some settings, are also 'suspect'—for example, those based upon national origin, alienage, indigency, or illegitimacy." See Stewart's concurrence in San Antonio Independent School District v. Rodriguez, 411 U.S. 61 and accompanying footnotes.

62. Compare Massiah v. United States, 377 U.S. 201 (1964), with Kirby v. Illinois, 406 U.S. 682 (1972).

63. See Chimel v. California, 395 U.S. 752 (1969), Coolidge v. New Hampshire, 403 U.S. 443 (1971), and Almeida-Sanchez v. United States, 413 U.S. 266 (1973), in which Stewart's Court or plurality opinions met a dissent from Justice White. On the other hand, see Camara v. Municipal Court, 387 U.S. 523 (1967).

64. Branzburg v. Hayes, 408 U.S. 665 (1972) (the newsman's-privilege case); Lloyd Corp. v. Tanner, 407 U.S. 551 (1972) (the shopping-center case); Laird v. Tatum, 408 U.S. 1 (1972) (the surveillance case). The differences continued into the 1972 term. See Miller v. California, 413 U.S. 15 (1973), Paris Adult Theatre I v. Slayton, 413 U.S. 49 (1973), and Pittsburg Press v. Pittsburg Comm. on Human Relations, 413 U.S. 376 (1973).

65. United States v. Kras, 409 U.S. 434, 457 (1973) (the bankruptcy-fee case); Butz v. Glover Livestock Comm., 411 U.S. 182, 189 (1973) (the "insignificant" case); Pittsburg Press v. Pittsburg Comm. on Human Relations, 413 U.S. 376, 402 (1973) (the newspaper-regulation case).

66. Simon, *supra*, note 1, p. 175.

67. Wyman v. James, 400 U.S. 309 (1971); Palmer v. Thompson, 403 U.S. 217, 228 (Blackmun, J., con-

curring); Dunn v. Blumstein, 405 U.S. 330, 360 (Blackmun, J., concurring in the result); United States v. Kras, 409 U.S. 434 (1973).

68. Eisenstadt v. Baird, 405 U.S. 438, 472 (1972) (Burger, C. J., dissenting).

69. "Law and the 'Burger-Nixon' Court," *The New York Times,* August 9, 1972.

70. The cases mentioned in this paragraph as demonstrating Chief Justice Burger's and Justice Blackmun's differing positions are, respectively, James v. Valtierra, 402 U.S. 137 (1971); Committee for Pub. Educ. & Relig. Liberty v. Nyquist, 413 U.S. 756 (1973); Dunn v. Blumstein, 405 U.S. 330 (1972); Vlandis v. Kline, 412 U.S. 441 (1973).

71. United States v. United States District Court, 407 U.S. 297 (1972); Keyes v. Denver School District, 413 U.S. 189 (1973).

72. Sierra Club v. Morton, 405 U.S. 727, 760 (1972) (Blackmun, J., dissenting).

73. *Time,* November 12, 1973.

INDEX

Index

199

Index

Index

and politics of Supreme Court,
95
Prayer Breakfast Speech (1972),
100–3
on public school busing, 76
regionalism, lack of, 116–17
research, quality of, 47
reserve of, 118–20
in Richmond, Virginia, 85–86
schedule of, 43–44
scholarship of, 92–93
on school desegregation, *Keyes v.
Denver School District,* 75–76
on segregation, racial, 120–21
and social changes of '60s, 105
and speedy trials *(Columbia Law
Review),* 98
and sports, 112–13
staff, social life with, 113–14
staff and chambers of, 16
as Supreme Court Justice, life of,
114–15
on traditional social values,
107–8
as traditionalist, 105
Wilkinson, acceptance of, 9
and wiretapping of domestic
radicals, 100–2
workload, staff, division of, 46
on workload, Supreme Court,
79–86
as youth, description of, 112–13
Powers, separation of, 29
Precedent, legal, Powell's view of,
118
Precedent, in Supreme Court, 96
Press, 97
criticism of Supreme Court, 98
decisions, Supreme Court, re-
porting of, 97
Prison administration, 21
Privacy, right to, 60
Public discussion, of Supreme
Court, 19
Public dissent, 101–2
Public notables, gallery of, 49
Public opinion, influence on Su-
preme Court, 151–52
Public opinion, and Supreme Court
rulings, 20, 96–97

R
Racial discrimination, "invisible,"
134

(See also Segregation)
Racial minorities, and Justice Stew-
art, 167
Rather, Dan, 37
Reapportionment ruling, Daniel
Broder on, 140
Warren Court rulings, 137–39
Redskins, Washington, 14, 112
Rehnquist, Justice William, ix
on clerks' role and influence, Su-
preme Court, 56–57
in conference, 41
as former clerk, 49
and Justice Frankfurter, 37
as Nixon appointee, 157–58
nomination and confirmation,
Supreme Court, 9
Reich, Charles, 51
Research, clerk of Supreme Court,
63–64
Reston, James, 97–98
Reynolds v. Sims, 138
Richardson, Elliot, 177
as former clerk, Supreme Court,
49
Richmond, Department of Public
Works, 77
Richmond News Leader, 77
Richmond Times-Dispatch, 100, 101
Rights, Bill of, 4
Rinzler, Carol, xiv
Rockefeller, Nelson, 139
Rodak, Michael, 36, 45
Rodriguez, Demetrio, 27
Roth v. United States, 89
Rothesay Rebels, 113

S
Saltzburg, Stephen, xiv
*San Antonio Independent School District
v. Rodriguez,* 165
School, public school, segregation
in, 161–62
School desegregation, 132
(See also Segregation)
Brown v. Board of Education,
130–33
School prayers, 94
Scott, Dred, 64
Searches and seizures (Fourth
Amendment), 93
and Justice Black, 98
Security, national, and *United States
v. United States District Court,* 101

203

Index

ABOUT THE AUTHOR

J. Harvie Wilkinson III served as a law clerk to Supreme Court Justice Lewis F. Powell, Jr., during the 1971 and 1972 terms. He is now an Assistant Professor of Law at the University of Virginia, where he teaches courses in Federal Courts, Criminal Procedure, and a seminar in Constitutional Law. A Phi Beta Kappa and Magna Cum Laude graduate of Yale University in 1967, Mr. Wilkinson attended the University of Virginia Law School, where he was on the law review and was elected to Order of the Coif. In 1970 he was the Republican candidate for Congress in Virginia's Third Congressional District and was appointed by Governor Linwood Holton to the Board of Visitors of the University of Virginia, the youngest person ever to serve on that body. Mr. Wilkinson has written one previous book, *Harry Byrd and the Changing Face of Virginia Politics*, published by the University Press of Virginia in 1968, as well as articles for legal and historical periodicals.